Innovating Teaching

Ľudmila Adamová
Petra Muráriková (eds.)

Innovating Teaching and Learning

Reports from University Lecturers

Budrich UniPress Ltd.
Opladen • Berlin • Toronto 2013

A CIP catalogue record for this book is available from
Die Deutsche Bibliothek (The German Library)

© 2013 by Budrich UniPress Ltd. Opladen, Berlin & Toronto
www.budrich-unipress.eu

ISBN   978-3-86388-034-7 (Paperback)
eISBN 978-3-86388-194-8 (eBook)

Das Werk einschließlich aller seiner Teile ist urheberrechtlich geschützt. Jede Verwertung außerhalb der engen Grenzen des Urheberrechtsgesetzes ist ohne Zustimmung des Verlages unzulässig und strafbar. Das gilt insbesondere für Vervielfältigungen, Übersetzungen, Mikroverfilmungen und die Einspeicherung und Verarbeitung in elektronischen Systemen.

Die Deutsche Bibliothek – CIP-Einheitsaufnahme
Ein Titeldatensatz für die Publikation ist bei Der Deutschen Bibliothek erhältlich.

Budrich UniPress Ltd.
Stauffenbergstr. 7. D-51379 Leverkusen Opladen, Germany

86 Delma Drive. Toronto, ON M8W 4P6 Canada
www.budrich-unipress.eu

Jacket illustration by disegno, Wuppertal, Germany – www.disenjo.de
Typographical editing: Ulrike Weingärtner, Gründau, Germany
Printed in Europe on acid-free paper by paper&tinta, Warsaw, Poland

Table of Contents

Section 5: Making Assessment an Effective Tool for Student Learning

1. Innovating University Courses: Introduction

Ľudmila Adamová and Petra Muráriková

Becoming a student-oriented teacher who fosters growth and development in students is a process that matures over time and arises from experience. It is not always a direct process that instantly bears fruit, but is sometimes rather a sort of struggle with one's own expectations about the nature of the teaching profession, the needs, motivation and attitudes of students. For teachers it is necessary, therefore, to wittingly enhance the process of one's own professional and personal growth as well as the motivation for doing so, in order to improve the process of teaching and allow it to work more effectively towards students' florescence.

The effort to guide the teaching and learning process of both novice teachers and more experienced lecturers in higher education is mirrored in the book you hold in your hands. The idea centred at its heart is a firm conviction about the necessity of active and creative contributions of teachers to students' development and progress. Perceiving the wide-spread teaching-centred approach as inadequate and therefore failing in realization of this conviction, the authors of the book discuss various ways of revitalizing this ideal. Presenting the design, implementation and outcomes of their teaching innovations, contributing teachers share their experience that even small innovative teaching projects may result in promoting desired student learning.

The book discusses some of the most frequent teaching challenges as faced by ten Ph.D. Students and young university teachers. These challenges include lack of student motivation and engagement, large differences in skills and knowledge among students in a class, the need to help students to see relation between theory and practice and many others. The teachers reacted to these challenges by designing and implementing teaching innovations. Under teaching innovation we mean a change in teaching and student learning that followed principles of student-centred education, was inspired by pedagogical theory and was aimed to enhance student learning.

Each chapter offers a unique approach to addressing some of these problems by providing a detailed description of the pedagogical challenge, the method of the innovation plan based on pedagogical theory, the steps of its implementation and a discussion of the innovation's results. This way, the readers can be provided with inspiration through step-by-step suggestions for implementing the innovative elements into their own teaching and student learning and enriched by the inclusion of many useful suggestions for successful application.

All of the authors first trained at the summer school *Teaching and Learning in Higher Education* which took place in Piešťany and Moravany nad Váhom (Slovakia) during two terms: 3-11 July and 14-22 August 2011. The school was organized by the Centre for Development of Ph.D. Candidates, Institute of Physics, Slovak Academy of Sciences for beginner teachers from various universities in Slovakia. The purpose of the school was to help teachers to enhance their teaching and student learning by 1) making teachers more student-centred in their practice, 2) improving their capacity to critically reflect on their own courses and 3) developing their capability to apply pedagogical theory. By student-centeredness it is implied here that teachers should focus more on how their students learn rather than placing importance on their own performance as teachers (Biggs and Tang 2007: 19, O'Neill and mcmahon 2005: 27-29).

The summer school was followed by a one-year program entitled *Inquiry into Student Learning* that consisted of implementing and evaluating teaching innovations based on the knowledge and skills acquired during the summer school. Participants from the summer school who were teaching a course in the following semester were invited to enrol also in this follow-up program. Those 26 teachers who accepted the invitation were innovating their teaching and student learning under the supervision of four professional teacher developers who served as coaches, including Christine Rabl (from University of Vienna), Joanna Renc-Roe, and Mátyás Szabó (from Central European University in Budapest) and Eszter Simon (from the Institute of Physics, Slovak Academy of Sciences).

The program included the design of a pedagogical innovation and a new syllabus reflecting the desired change in teaching and learning, the implementation of the teaching innovation during one semester including collecting evidence about student learning, the presentation of the innovation's results and a revision of the teacher's own statement of teaching philosophy. Both the summer school and the teacher inquiry program were funded through a three-year grant provided by the European Social Fund.

This publication presents the best reports of the program participants' research into student learning, as recommended by the coaches in the program. The innovation projects were carried out between September 2011 and September 2012. The purpose of the book is to provide an example for university teachers considering change in their courses. Moreover, it could be useful for students of Pedagogy at both the undergraduate and postgraduate level who study teaching and learning in higher education. In addition, it could be a source of inspiration for academics and researchers teaching and training students of pedagogy and serve as a guidebook for all beginner and more experienced teachers facing similar challenges during their teaching practice.

This book is a successor of two books already published by Budrich unipress called *IT in Action. Stimulating Quality Learning at Undergraduate Students* (2010) edited by Gabriela Pleschová and *Teaching Theory and Academic Writing. A Guide to Undergraduate Lecturing in Political Science* (2008) edited by Malte Brosig and Kinga Kas. However, since the book covers teaching academic courses of a broad variety (including Ethics, History, Journalism, Linguistics, Medicine, Biology, Economics etc.), it is hoped to be interesting and useful for a far larger readership.

The content of the book is divided into five sections reflecting the character of the innovation. The first section – *Improving student pre-class preparation* – starts with the chapter written by Ľudmila Adamová. Her teaching innovation was based on applying the just-in-time teaching and learning method which resulted in students' regular preparation for the seminars as well as in their greater involvement in class activities and subject matter.

In the following chapter, Marek Živčák offers inspiration for teachers with very limited possibilities for introducing teaching and learning changes into the classroom. The innovation, aimed at improving students' pre-class preparation through use of self-scoring on-line quizzes, tried to address the problem of a lack of background and basic knowledge of the first year science students. The author demonstrates how students of the innovated course improved their pre-class preparation as well as their in-class learning.

Katarína Hrnčiarová presents other ways of dealing with students' insufficient preparation for seminars as well as for the final examination. Inspired by theory of student motivation, she decided to engage students in blog writing, which resulted not only in an increase of students' activity in the seminars, but above all in the improvement of their critical thinking.

The second section of the book discusses the issue of *teaching large classes*. In her chapter, Petra Muráriková discusses the possibility of using blended learning as a tool to develop skills and increase student motivation. Showing some surprising results, the author challenges the all-powerful motivational potential frequently attributed to virtual teaching as well as the use of modern technologies, talking up instead the necessity for personal, vital relationships between teacher and students.

Peter Dzurjaník, on the other hand, demonstrates that deeper involvement of students in the subject matter through engagement in problem solving groups secures better understanding of the topics and can increase students' activity and motivation.

Contributions in the third section deal with the challenge *of teaching courses rich in complex terminology*. Adriana Boleková reports on the results of the innovation in teaching based on the usage of mnemonics and imagination, which ultimately led not only to the increase of students' in-class activity, but also to improved learning outcomes.

Martina Lučkaničová, the author of the second chapter in this section, discusses the prospects of teaching a course rich in complex terminology, in an interesting and attention-catching way. Besides presenting the positive effect of the innovation, the author also shares her experience with teaching two diverse groups of students and discusses ways of overcoming an intolerant atmosphere prevailing in one of them.

The fourth section tries to address the challenge of *enhancing student abilities of theory application*. Anna Vallušová's chapter touches mainly on the challenge of passive and surface student learning. By implementing tools for encouraging active learning, the author aimed at improving student knowledge and its application. Following the suggestions from some prominent teachers, she offers concrete steps for implementing an innovative approach that resulted in students acquiring the desired level of subject mastery.

The last section of the book brings reflections on *making assessment an effective tool for student learning*. Terézia Repáňová focuses on the change of the assessment criteria according to Bloom's taxonomy. She addressed two main teaching challenges: weak student motivation and the change of the traditional assessment criteria, which in light of stated objectives proved to be insufficient. As a result of her innovation, the students' motivation increased and they made visible progress to more complex cognitive processes.

In the final chapter Miroslava Petáková discusses the possibilities for student motivation and class restructuring. An increase in students' activity and interest in the subject together with a comparative analysis of students' results before and after the innovation serve as evidence that the implementation of changes was successful.

To conclude, it is the editors' hope that the readers will find this book a source of inspiration for introducing changes into their courses for the benefit of their students.

References

Biggs, J./Tang, C. (2007): Teaching for Quality Learning at University: What the Student does. 3rd edition. Maidenhead: Society for Research Into Higher Education and Open University Press.

O'Neill, G./mcmahon, T. (2005): "Student-centered Learning. What does it Mean for Students and Lecturers." In: O'Neill, Geraldine/mcmahon, Tim. (eds.): Emerging Issues in the Practice of University Learning and Teaching. Dublin: AISHE, pp. 27-36, 21 November 2012, www.aishe.org/readings/2005-1/oneill-mcmahon-Tues_19th_Oct_SCL.pdf.

Acknowledgement

This publication was supported by the European Union and the European Social Fund. Modern education for the knowledge-based society/Project is co-financed from EU resources.

Európska únia
Európsky sociálny fond

Operačný program
VZDELÁVANIE

Section 1: Improving Student Pre-class Preparation

2. Using Just-In-Time Teaching to Encourage Students' Regular Pre-Class Preparation

Ľudmila Adamová, Constantine the Philosopher University in Nitra

2.1 Introduction

This paper discusses the challenges of innovating the seminars on Contemporary English Language, a compulsory course which is a part of the MA program in Translation Studies. The course requires a high level of knowledge comprehension, and by the end of the course students are expected to 1) remember and understand stylistic devices and expressive means and 2) analyse various kinds of texts, including identifying their style and register. Moreover, as students of Translation Studies, they are expected to apply acquired knowledge in the comparative analysis of the original text and its translation.

In the academic year 2011/2012 the seminar was attended by 38 students, who were divided into three groups. Since the course consisted of seminars and lectures, it combined two basic methods of teaching: lecturing and discussions on assigned topics as well as practical text analysis in seminars. In spite of the fact that in previous years students regularly received good marks in the final test, as the seminar leader I was struggling with a problem of students' insufficient preparation for the seminars. Moreover, I could notice that in the final test students usually relied on memorizing the definitions and not on their understanding.

Traditionally, students were expected to attend lectures to familiarize themselves with the theory and apply the theory by means of practical analysis of the texts in the seminars and in their written essays. However, a lot of them did not attend the lectures regularly and did not read the compulsory literature. Therefore, before innovating this course, much time had to be spent with introduction and explanation of the theory at the beginning of the each seminar because students usually were not able to analyse the texts due to the missing theoretical background. Because of students' insufficient preparation before the seminar, very few students actively participated in the seminar. In order to overcome this problem, the method called *just-in-time teaching* was applied.

The results of the innovation were evaluated by several means, including *minute papers* as well as a final test and in-depth analytical essays using some of the *open-ended questions* discussed at the seminar. While students' responses in minute papers were not included in the final assessment, because their purpose was to provide the teacher with immediate feedback on students' learning, the results from the final test and essays were a component of the final assessment.

2.2 Aims of the Innovation and Theoretical Background

The teaching innovation was a complex procedure that included not only the change of teaching methods, but also the innovation of the syllabus and the change of the assessment. First of all it was necessary to change the syllabus completely and elaborate all its parts in detail in order to set clear rules, requirements, and methods for students' assessment. As a result, students were given a ten-page syllabus instead of two pages given last term where they could find all the information related to the course, its purpose, character and goals.

As it was mentioned before, the major problem to solve was related to the students' insufficient pre-class preparation for the seminars. Considering *Bloom's taxonomy* as quoted in Atherton (2011), after introducing the innovation, students of the course were expected to comprehend the stylistic rules of English, apply them while analysing the texts, synthesize the results and comment on stylistic features of the analysed texts. Before the innovation, students had difficulty with the first step, i.e. Comprehension of stylistic theory. As a result of this, it was almost impossible for them to get to the higher steps in Bloom's taxonomy.

To address this challenge it was necessary to focus on the students' pre-class preparation by introducing the method of just-in-time teaching (jitt). According to Novak et al. (1999) the main purpose of this strategy is to increase the effectiveness of the classroom sessions, where a teacher and students are present. In general, it can be defined as a teaching and learning strategy based on the interaction between web-based study assignments and an active learner classroom. In jitt students are expected to respond electronically to assignments which are due before the seminar. Then the teacher can read the student submissions "just-in-time" to modify the class to suit the students' needs. Thus, in jitt the students' home preparation directly affects what happens during the seminars. Moreover, this pedagogic strategy

14

helps students achieve mastery by helping teachers engage students in their learning, and on the other hand it helps teachers to make the class setting more participatory and students stay focused and prepared to learn throughout the semester (Novak et al. 1999).

Applying the just-in-time teaching and learning method in this class, the literature for each seminar was assigned, which students had to read before the class, prepare answers to questions based on reading the texts and send it to the teacher via email before each seminar. Moreover, all seminars were divided into three main parts: a short theoretical survey, practical analysis and students' presentations. In the first part, i.e. A short theoretical survey, the focus was on checking the students' knowledge acquired from lectures and home preparation, i.e. Reading of the assigned chapters from the textbook. Students were assigned a set of questions to answer in the form of a minute paper, in other words, a *half-sheet response*, which, according to Angelo and Cross (1993: 148), provides a quick and extremely simple way to collect written feedback on student learning.

To use the minute paper, a teacher stops class two or three minutes before its end and asks students to respond briefly to questions focused on identifying the most important thing learned during the class as well as formulating questions which remained unanswered. Students write their responses on index cards or half-sheets of scrap paper and hand them in. As it is further stated, "the great advantage of minute papers is that they provide manageable amounts of timely and useful feedback for a minimal investment of time and energy. […] That feedback can help teachers decide whether any mid-course corrections or changes are needed and, if so, what kinds of instructional adjustments to make" (Angelo and Cross 1993: 148).

The minute papers were used to check to what extent students understood the subject matter. Most of the questions had the form of *closed-ended questions* that could be relatively easily answered when the student has read the literature, because the aim in this phase was to make students study assigned literature at home.

With the aim to motivate the students to prepare for the seminars, they were given three unexpected mini-tests based on the readings to check the level of their pre-class preparation. At the very beginning of the term the students were informed that these mini-tests would count towards their final grade, and the number of points allotted for each test was specified in the syllabus. Moreover, students were given at least one open-ended question which was later used to initiate the discussion where students could compare and discuss their opinions.

The purpose of the course was not only to provide essential theoretical knowledge, but also its practical application in text analysis. As a result, the second part of the seminars was dedicated to the practical exercises assigned for each of the seminars (the list of the exercises was included in the syllabus as well). Through these exercises students could test their theory comprehension and apply it using stylistic analysis at all language levels. Students were expected to work individually, in pairs or in small groups and later discuss their results with the rest of the class to get feedback from the teacher and from their peers. Moreover, students were asked to write essays as another form of home preparation. This had the form of an in-depth analytical essay concerning some of the open-ended questions discussed in the seminars. Furthermore, students were asked to work in pairs to prepare their own presentations on selected topics. The list of the topics was included in the syllabus as well.

Due to the slight discrepancy between the title of the course (Contemporary English Language) and its content (English stylistics), as well as students' expectations and needs related to their field of study, the innovation was not related only to teaching methods, but also to the course content, which was adapted to become more interdisciplinary, which is in accordance with the requirements and expectations set at the MA level of the Translation Studies. It was expected that the interdisciplinary approach could help students to develop and improve their translation skills as well as to increase their interest in the subject matter.

2.3 Research Design

The results of the teaching innovation were measured by seven indicators. All of them were related to the qualitative research design. Firstly, the progress and the development of students' skills and knowledge were checked regularly through weekly homework assignments. Moreover, direct feedback was provided almost every session through minute papers. Aside from this, as the seminar teacher, I could observe students' in-class activity as well as the level of their knowledge based on pre-class preparation. The students' essays and their oral presentations provided another indicator of the creative environment in the class and made students responsible for studying and for the content of the seminars – peer lecturing. Last but not least, the final test, which contained not only theoretical questions, but also practical tasks, documented the level of students' comprehension and application of theory.

As another research instrument, a student feedback questionnaire was used as well. Moreover, in the last seminar the students were asked to write a short reaction paper containing their anonymous reflection on the format and content of the course (36 out of 38 students submitted their reaction papers, i.e. Approximately 95%). Besides expressing their opinions on aforementioned topics, students were asked to propose topics which they would be interested to discuss in future seminars.

16

Concerning assessment, the combination of both types – *summative* as well as *formative assessment* – was used. Since students were given a task to prepare their own presentations, formative assessment was used to give students direct feedback. In addition, it was an opportunity to check and evaluate their progress in the process of learning stylistics during the semester. It was also a kind of feedback for the teacher to know to what extent students understood the theory and, consequently, whether they were able to apply it through practical analysis of the texts.

Summative assessment consisted of measuring the students' level of practical application of the knowledge they gained by home preparation, from the lecture and self-study using three short tests, the seminar works, as well as the final test at the end of the term.

2.4 Findings

The innovation resulted not only in an increase in students' activity, but, moreover, in an increase of their interest in the subject matter of the course. As a result, the innovation based on just-in-time teaching method was found useful. Since the students were given points for each of the homework assignments, they were encouraged to prepare for each class by reading the assigned literature and by applying their theoretical knowledge through practical analysis. As a result, they appeared substantially better prepared for each session when compared with the group taught the academic year before.

The students' reactions to different teaching and learning methods, for example group or pair discussion, presentations, etc. Were observed through the semester and analysed. Since more teaching methods were applied, it was possible to compare them and consider which of them worked more or less effectively. The innovation of the syllabus was found to be one of the most useful steps. Unfortunately, some students did not read the syllabus or did not read it thoroughly, which became apparent in their presentations. There was a pair of students who did not apply an interdisciplinary approach to their presentation. This was later explained as the result of not reading the syllabus properly. To avoid similar situations in the future, it seems advisable to read and comment on the syllabus in the first seminar at the beginning of the each term.

Regular homework also helped students to become more focused on the subject matter. Minute papers were good as a kind of feedback, but after being repeatedly used in several classes, they became less effective. The students knew they would not be given points for writing them, which was why some of them did not answer the questions properly. On the other hand, the mini-tests made students prepare regularly for the seminars, and it was possible to notice improvement in their results.

Moreover, the students' responses stated in the feedback questionnaire used in the last seminar were very inspiring, because a lot of new and interesting topics were proposed there which are planned be included into the content of the seminars next academic year.

Last but not least, the interdisciplinary approach to teaching stylistic analysis was found the most effective way how to increase students' motivation and to improve and develop their critical thinking. This kind of approach was applied in assigning students' presentations, in which they were asked not only to analyse the texts, but also to compare the originals and their translations. Since the students were asked to work in pairs, it also helped to improve their abilities to cooperate and to communicate with their colleagues, which can also be very important for their future career.

Figure 1: Comparison of students' results

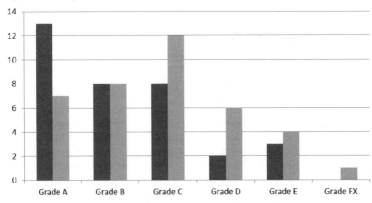

Source: own depiction

Interestingly, the innovation did not result in clear improvement of student learning outcomes as measured by the assessment results. Comparing the students' final grades with the previous academic year, fewer students received A grades (the highest grade on the ECTS scale). Out of 34 students who attended the course in the academic year 2010/2011, 13 students got an A, 8 students a B, 8 students a C, 2 students a D and 3 students an E. For comparison, out of 38 students who attended the course in the academic year 2011/2012, 7 students were given A grades, 8 students B grades, 12 students C grades, 6 students D grades, 4 students E grades and one student a grade of FX, i.e. Failed the course (see Figure 1). There was no change in the texts assigned for analysis and no change in the content and amount of the assigned readings. The only change was related to the teaching and learning methods, which probably made the course more demanding for the students.

As a result of this, it can be assumed that students who got grade A really deserved the best grade, because they had to study harder than the students the year before and their final assessment was not based solely on the memorizing of some theory for the final test. However, the data, as well as the assumption mentioned, is open to a lot of interpretations. The change in results of the final assessment may be related to the fact that different students attended the course than in the previous academic year and their level of skills and abilities before enrolling the course could have differed. On the other hand, another question may arise – whether proper teaching methods were chosen. This is the reason why there is a need for further research in this area to compare more student groups in order to learn which of the teaching methods is the most effective.

2.5 Limitations of the Study and Suggestions for Future Improvement

When teaching this course, some organizational problems were encountered. Some of the students broke the rules and submitted their homework after the deadline. When it happened for the first time, this homework was accepted. Afterwards, some students started to regularly submit their homework late and there was not enough time for the teacher to check it and prepare the feedback. That is why in the future students should be required to follow the rules, and any homework sent after the set deadline should not be accepted or they may have points taken off for its late delivery. This is very important not only for effective working of the just-in-time teaching method, but also for students to learn to respect the given rules.

2.6 Conclusion

This paper discussed the challenges of innovating the seminars on Contemporary English Language, a compulsory course which is a part of the MA program in Translation Studies. The teaching problem which was addressed included the problems related to insufficient pre-class preparation of the students and thus lack of their active participation in the seminars. In order to overcome the problem the method called just-in-time teaching was applied.

Using this teaching and learning method, the topics for each seminar were assigned and students had to study relevant theory before the class, prepare homework and send it to the teacher via email before each seminar. The innovation was found successful. Thanks to this regular home preparation the students were familiarized with the theory and they were able to apply their theoretical knowledge while doing practical stylistic analysis of given texts. By means of this strategy, as the seminar teacher, I could engage students in their learning. It and helped to make the class setting more participatory and students stay focused and prepared to learn throughout the semester. Thanks to the change in the final assessment, according to which the students were given points not only for their final test, but also for their work during the whole semester, their final assessment could be considered to be more appropriate and objective.

I appreciated the opportunity to attend the Summer School *Teaching and Learning in Higher Education* and the follow-up program, because it showed me the ways how to improve my teaching and student learning. The fact that I started to think about my teaching as a strategic and purposeful activity helped me to seek and find new ways that I can teach and make my seminars more interesting for the students and more effective in stimulating good learning in students. Before enrolling the program I thought that it was quite difficult to find new ways of teaching a linguistic discipline and I was sceptical about possibilities of its innovation. During the one-year program I learned it is possible as I could see that I can achieve a meaningful change and increase the students' interest in the subject matter by means of topics which they find useful and applicable in their future work and by means of regular preparation which is based not only on theoretical knowledge, but also on its practical application.

References

Angelo, T. A/Cross, K. P. (1993): Classroom Assessment Techniques. San Francisco: Jossey-Bass.

Atherton, J. S. (2011): "Learning and Teaching; Bloom's Taxonomy." 19 April 2012, www.learningandteaching.info/learning/bloomtax.htm.

Novak, G./Gavrin, A./Christian, W./Patterson, E. (1999): Just-In-Time Teaching: Blending Active Learning with Web Technology. Upper Saddle River: Prentice Hall.

Just-in-Time-Teaching (1999-2006): 19 April 2012, http://jittdl.physics.iupui.edu/jitt/#.

3. Self-scoring Online Quizzes as a Tool for Enhancement of Student Reading and Comprehension

Marek Živčák, Slovak University of Agriculture in Nitra

3.1 Introduction

The aim of this paper is to share experiences regarding the improvement of teaching aimed at out-of-class activities using available e-learning tools. The main teaching challenge identified was the low fundamental knowledge of students attending the classes, leading to insufficient comprehension and hence to surface learning without understanding of the topic. The main effort was directed towards improving students' preparation through assigned readings and comprehension of these through compulsory, self-scoring online quizzes. This reduced the time necessary for in-class lecturing, which was used for other motivating activities. The effect of the innovation was measured by the comparison of mid-term exam results of the tested group with a similar group's results from the previous year. The limits of presented approach as well as possible ways of its further improvement are outlined below.

The course Plant Physiology is a compulsory part of the bachelor's degree for different specializations within the study of Agriculture or Biology in the first or, mostly, second year. The course has a long and continuous history (several decades) and is very well established. Having a rather conservative design, it is innovated mainly by modern technical equipment, but not so much by modern pedagogical approaches.

The format, time schedule, content and formal assessment of the course are strictly set by the guarantors of the discipline (professors), who also deliver lectures as well as prepare the final test and examine students at the end of semester. The most important parts of the course are the classes with small groups of usually less than twenty students, taught by assistant professors or Ph.D. Students. Throughout the initial eleven weeks, the classes are comprised mostly of laboratory experiments, with some time reserved for presentation of theory as an addition to the lectures. This is aimed mostly at some practical aspects directly associated with the theory presented in lectures. There is also some limited time for discussions or additional explanations of problematic issues. The last two classes are reserved for traditional seminars, where the students present their papers on particular topics, followed by discussion.

Five years' experience with teaching the subject led me to the observation of the students' generally poor level of fundamental knowledge of biology, as well as a low intrinsic motivation to study the subject. This was probably caused by the fact that the majority of students do not study Biology as their major and the course is in the initial part of their curricula. The subject is enormously rich in terminology, and without previous knowledge of context and terminology, students often lose the narrative thread and hence, many of them are not able to understand the issues explained. It is, however, almost impossible to familiarize oneself with this discipline without deep understanding of the main mechanisms of plant function.

Probably as a result of this lack of basic knowledge, students tend to use surface learning instead of a deep learning approach (Ramsden 1992). This is reflected in practice by students' almost complete lack of interest in asking questions, thinking critically about the topic, or examining the context of the problem. During the course, the role of student's engagement, however, should change from newcomer to co-operator or collaborator, and finally to initiator or partner. This requires experienced guidance on the part of the instructor, as these active roles are not intuitive for many adult learners. Several years of personal experience support the findings that students often feel more comfortable in passive roles (see also Conrad and Donaldson 2004).

In general, the results of scientific studies, as well as the exchange of personal experiences in the teaching community, offer many possible ways of improving teaching towards increasing the motivation of students to learn. However, the practical and successful application strongly depends on the type of discipline, intrinsic motivation, students' level of knowledge, as well as other factors.

One of the most significant determining factors is the level of "freedom" in teaching, in terms of competences to organize the time and content of classes. As different sections of the classes are taught by several teachers, the content (curriculum and syllabus) of the classes is more or less strictly determined, with very little time available for additional activities. Therefore, the possibilities to improve students' learning through in-class activities are very limited; however, even in the case of having very limited options for modifying the content, design of learning units, or assessment, there are still some possibilities to perform efficient tools leading to enhanced students' learning.

In summary, for improving of students' comprehension and hence, increasing their engagement and motivation, it was necessary to improve their fundamental knowledge before the class. For this reason, the attention was focused on out-of-class activities.

3.2 Aims of the Innovation and Theoretical Background

Drawing on the identified teaching challenge, the main objective of the innovation was to introduce an external motivation for students to read assigned texts before each class in order to familiarize themselves with the topic and terminology used throughout the course. This aimed to lead to better preparation of students coming to class and hence to improve their comprehension of the content and the contexts of the topic. Because I believe that the most efficient way of teaching is to maintain a relaxed and friendly atmosphere, the stated aim was planned to be achieved without examining students and other 'stressful events' during the classes. Therefore, the self-study and self-scoring assessment was introduced as a part of students' out of class preparation.

This was done in accordance with the principle of mcalpine (2004: 119), who proposed a model of teaching and learning based on more practice in class and more information out of class. It brings the opportunity to discuss the issues in class in-depth, to get feedback from the others, and to recognize that much 'informing' can be done independently. The class time can be structured to support a *deep approach* to learning by drawing the attention of students through engaging activities or discussion led in a challenging way.

For out of class activities, technology-enhanced learning techniques were used, especially a virtual learning environment. The combination of conventional teaching with e-learning is called *blended learning* (Garrison and Kanuka 2004: 95). It represents an opportunity to fundamentally redesign the approach to teaching and learning, so that higher educational institutions may benefit from increased effectiveness, convenience and efficiency (Garrison and Vaughan 2008: 13).

This approach consists of four phases: (a) before face-to-face, (b) face-to-face, (c) after face-to-face and (d) preparation for the next face-to-face session. A similar structure can be observed in the innovated design of this course (see Figure 2): the first and last phase represent reading and on-line testing, the second phase is the personal contact in class, and the third phase represents other learning activities outside of class, mainly protocols from experiments, short homework assignments and writing the seminar paper. This new learning design replaced the previous class format based on in-class explanations of basic definitions and additional lecturing without out-of-class preparation of students.

In the practical application of this innovation, emphasis was put on the reading material available for students in electronic form on the web (LMS Moodle). The prepared texts contained the main topic associated with the following class, including definitions of key terms and descriptions of the students answered questions referring to the readings.

Figure 2: The design of learning unit before the innovation (previous state) and after innovation (recent state).

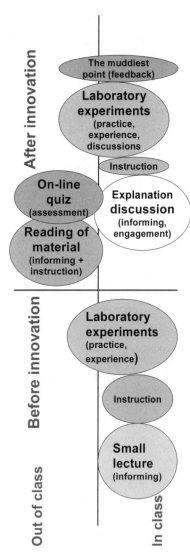

Source: own depiction

24

Main processes. The readings were connected with on-line quizzes, in which The quizzes were compulsory and passing them (level of 80% and more) was required for attending the following class. Students had as many attempts as they needed to pass the quiz. For each attempt, the Moodle created an original quiz with unique sequence of questions and unique sequence of a-b-c-d-e-f answers (this type of quiz questions was the most frequent). Quizzes were self-scoring; hence, the checking of the results took only several minutes before the class. The number and formulation of questions made it almost impossible to pass the quiz without reading the text.

Even though this system did not have ambitions to make students able to reproduce the topic they read, it was expected that students would come to class informed and the level of comprehension would increase. A similar approach of using on-line quizzes outside of class to increase student engagement in class was successfully applied by Cashman and Eschenbach (2003) in the teaching of an Environmental Engineering course.

A feedback activity called the muddiest point was also applied (Angelo and Cross 1993: 154). The students were asked to write briefly on a sheet of paper what they did not understand. The papers were collected before the end of the class and the responses were discussed immediately or at the next class, depending on the time remaining.

In all groups in which the innovation was applied, no technical problems or problems with internet access were reported. Compared to the state of affairs from few years ago, this time all students were well familiarized with computers and the internet, and the reactions to activities requiring the use of Information Technology were generally positive.

3.3 Research Design

The effect of the method applied was measured by comparing students' mid-term test results with student results from previous year (2010). In 2010, 39 students divided into two groups (39.4% men, 60.6% women) and in 2011, 31 students again divided into two groups (38.7% men, 61.3% women) were included; all of them were students of the same Faculty and specialization (students of Agriculture). The same set of tests for the mid-semester exam was used both years. The evaluation measured (a) average test results (in %) and (b) the distribution of grades (A to FX), according to the scores obtained on the test.

Moreover, an additional analysis of student's out-of-class activity was completed, depending on the fact whether the activity (quiz) was compulsory or voluntary. The tested group was compared with a group taught by another teacher. Both groups had the same access to Moodle (compulsory in both groups) and to quizzes; however, the use of the quizzes in other teacher's group was voluntary (students were encouraged to use the quizzes as an effective tool to improve their knowledge). The percentage of students accessing the quizzes, completing the quiz, and passing the quiz (with a score of 80%) was evaluated.

The evaluation of the innovation was done according to *Gibbs reflective cycle* (Gibbs, 1988), based on feelings (subjective perception), evaluation (of students' results and knowledge), analysis (searching for reasons), action plan (outline and start of innovation) and description (what happened after the innovation started) followed again by feelings, evaluation (for example by the subjective and objective evaluation of the effects of the innovation, followed by identification of limitations and suggestions for the future), etc.

3.4 Findings

The quantitative analysis of mid-term exam results showed only slight improvement (Figure 3a and 3b). Almost no significant increase in average percentage (Figure 3a), indicating noticeable total improvement of students' results was observed. However, as this parameter can be strongly influenced by the extremes (for example, by the poor results of a few individuals), the distribution of results according to the grades (Figure 3b) was also analysed. Within this, an increase of the best grades (A and B), which were not present in 2010, can be observed. Moreover, while in 2010 the largest group of students did not pass the course (receiving a grade of FX), in 2011 the group of students who received the grade E became the dominant one.

Figure 3a: Comparison of average result (in%) of mid-term exam recorded in assessed groups in 2010 (before the start of innovation) and in 2011 (after the innovation). Error bars represent standard deviation ($P = 0.95$).

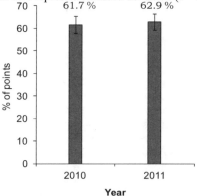

Source: own depiction

*Figure 3b:*Distribution of grades according to the percentage obtained on the mid-term exam in 2010 and 2011.

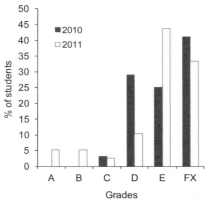

Source: own depiction

Despite the fact that the results may be challenged, the subjective observations confirmed the positive effect of the applied innovation. Firstly, more students were answering the questions asked in class correctly. Secondly, a better comprehension of specific terminology was observed. Thirdly, the assumption that the improvement of fundamental knowledge would also increase student engagement and motivation in class was partly fulfilled: there was unfortunately still a majority of students remaining in their passive roles.

Figure 4: Comparison of attendance and results of two groups of students with compulsory and voluntary form of the same self-scoring quizzes.

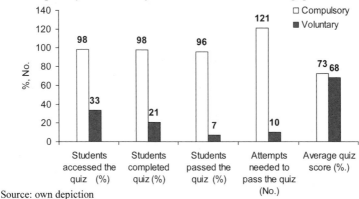

Source: own depiction

The question to be discussed is whether the self-scoring quizzes would be efficient if used as a voluntary activity. The comparison of the voluntary and compulsory approaches brought clear findings (Figure 4).

The results show that, in the group where the task was compulsory, almost all students (98%) accessed, completed and passed the quizzes, while most of the students in the group with quizzes as a voluntary task did not access the quizzes. Only 33% of students in that group accessed the quiz, 21% of students completed the quiz, and only 7% of students passed the test. The only comparable parameter in both groups was the average test results percentage of the few active students who voluntarily attended the quizzes and scored relatively well. Since creating the quizzes is a rather difficult and time-consuming task, based on the results, it can be claimed that creating the quizzes which are voluntary seems to be a pointless waste of time.

3.5 Limitations of the Study and Suggestions for Future Improvement

Although students achieved better results in terms of the distribution of grades, the results were not as expected. Several interpretations come into consideration. Firstly, it could be influenced by improper timing in 2011; the mid-term exam was delayed, and there was a time gap between the students doing quizzes and taking the exam. Secondly, the exam was scheduled during the "Student Fest Week" of that year. As there was a lot of entertainment in that week, some students were less concentrated on their studies. These interpretations could be, however, partly attributed to methodical part of the assessment. As the results of only one year were evaluated, one accidental factor could completely influence the results.

Nevertheless, other problems that occurred merit attention. To start with, some students evidently "bypassed" the system. Probably the most frequent method was collective work, whereby some skilled students helped other students, who did not read the text, to pass the quizzes. On these students, therefore, the innovation had only a negligible impact. To solve this problem, these groups of students can be detected by the time and duration of the quiz; such information is easily accessible to the teacher in Moodle.

Additionally, despite a more or less positive attitude towards quizzes, students considered the provided texts to be rather boring. The used texts were scanned from an available textbook (in Slovak language) and provided as PDF files. However, there are not enough attractive, suitable and available texts in Slovak which could be used for this purpose. This could be another factor that influenced the success of the innovation, and it clearly draws an area for further improvement.

Therefore, a crucial step for more successful application of the proposed innovation could be the preparation of new texts that would be more attractive, demonstrative, and easily readable for students. Subsequently, the quizzes would have to be adjusted to the new text. In addition, it would be more effective if more questions in the quizzes would be focused on the application of knowledge instead of simple definitions.

When focusing on tools provided by the blended learning approach, the reading and self-assessment quizzes were the integrative part of the before face-to-face phase. However, it is only one of the possibilities proposed by Garrison and Vaughan (2008: 113). Also very promising are podcasting or video tools for communication between teacher and students. The advantages of these tools are that they allow students to listen and view the course-related material outside of class time, at their own pace as often as required to increase understanding.

A part which also could be incorporated into teaching is the phase containing post face-to-face activities (Garisson and Vaughan, 2008: 127), which could be aimed mainly on discussions, writing essays, etc. However, it would require much deeper engagement and intrinsic motivation of students than it could be achieved this time. Anyway, there is still the possibility to apply feedback in a form of the muddiest point as proposed by Angelo and Cross (1993: 154) by the e-tools of LMS Moodle.

Similarly, the time spared by less lecturing can be eventually used for some alternative activities. Instead of transmission of information during class, other approaches could be applied (Garisson and Vaughan 2008: 118). For example, the anonymous results of quizzes could be presented to students, and the questions from the quiz could be discussed. Another possibility would be to apply a kind of *just-in-time teaching*, where the quizzes would enable the teacher to identify the problematic issues shortly before class. Thus, such an issue could be included into the content of the class (Novak et al. 1999). All these ideas remain open for the future.

Furthermore, e-learning offers many more possibilities than just on-line assessment. Garrison and Vaughan (2008: 13) introduced the model of *Community of Inquiry* used both in distance and blended learning. This concept is based on three pillars: the Social Presence enables students to identify with the community by projecting their individual personalities; the Cognitive Presence enables the development of the students' critical thinking through the sustained reflection of the community; and the Teaching Presence enables the direction of cognitive and social processes for the purpose of realizing personally meaningful and educationally worthwhile learning outcomes.

This, however, requires a high level of effort connected to organizing and directing on-line discussion. Although such forms of communication can hardly become dominant in natural sciences (they are useful mainly in humanities), some of their aspects are worth considering; mostly those aimed at the development of logical thinking through solving "challenging issues" including some kind of on-line competitions and guided on-line discussion of interesting tasks.

Although there are many opportunities for improvement of teaching this course, the change of the content and assessment rules is considered to carry the highest potential. Such changes could be much more efficient than previously applied or suggested approaches, as the discipline can become more interesting and popular for many students. Moreover, some alternative forms of formative assessment, as well as other approaches engaging to learn (well discussed in Renc-Roe 2006) can be more motivating compared to the more or less conservative system based only on simple summative assessment in the form of written exams.

Despite the large number of areas for improvement, these activities had led to many new experiences and ideas, which resulted in the encouragement to continue with innovating activities, including some new approaches for future teaching.

3.6 Conclusion

The innovative project presented in this chapter was aimed at the improvement of teaching the course Plant Physiology, a subject taught as a compulsory part of curricula of undergraduate programs of Agricultural studies. One of the most important challenges of teaching and learning that were identified was the low level of comprehension caused by insufficient prior knowledge and poor intrinsic motivation of students to prepare for the course. This led to predominantly surface learning and poor results for the majority of students.

Because of limited competences for substantial re-organization of in-class activities, the emphasis was placed on out-off class preparation of students using virtual learning environment (LMS Moodle). The aim of the innovation was to stimulate students to read the assigned texts in order to increase the level of their knowledge necessary for understanding the topic of classes. The tools of external motivation to read the texts were compulsory, self-scoring online quizzes. This model was realized in accordance with mcalpine's (2004) theoretical principle based on efforts to introduce more practice in the classroom and more information transfer outside of class.

The shift of activities from class to home brought also a side effect in the form of saving time previously used for frontal lecturing. The gained time advantage was instead used for informal teaching activities like discussions, small group activities, or more detailed explanation, if requested by students.

The comparison of grades in the experimental group and the group from the previous year showed only small improvement; however, the distribution of grades as well as the subjective perception of the teacher was rather positive. It was found that some students were better able to understand new topics, and some of them were able to explain even very difficult issues: it was evident that they read the assigned text carefully and with interest. However, this was valid only for a group of active students as it was shown by analysis of grades, which uncovered some areas for further improvement.

The strengths of the innovation were, among others, grounded in the easy operation and control through the internet, saving time usually spent explaining or examining in class, and the efficient utilization of this time for motivating activities. The weak points were the possibilities to bypass the system and the lack of suitable texts in the Slovak language. The theoretical knowledge as well as the experiences gained during the innovation can be useful particularly for further improvement and increasing the quality of teaching and learning process.

References

Angelo, T./Cross, P. (1993): Classroom Assessment Techniques: A Handbook for College Teachers. San Francisco: Jossey-Bass.

Cashman, E. M./Eschenbach, E. A. (2003): Using on-line quizzes outside the classroom to increase student engagement inside the classroom. American Society for Engineering Education. 16 October 2012, http://jittdl.physics.iupui.edu/jitt/cashman.html.

Conrad R. M./Donaldson J. A. (2004): Engaging the online learner. San Francisco: Jossey-Bass.

Garrison, D. R./Kanuka, H. (2004): "Blended learning: Uncovering its transformative potential in higher education." The Internet and Higher Education, 7, 2, pp. 95-105.

Garrison, D. R./Vaughan, N. D. (2008): Blended Learning in Higher Education: Framework, Principles, and Guidelines. San Francisco: Jossey-Bass.

Gibbs, G. (1988): Learning by Doing: A Guide to Teaching and Learning Methods. Oxford: Further Education Unit, Oxford Polytechnic.

Mcalpine, L. (2004): "Designing learning as well as teaching." Active Learning in Higher Education, 5, 2, pp. 119-134.

Novak, G. M./Patterson, E. T./Gavrin, A. D./Christian, W. (1999): Just-in-time teaching: Blending active learning with Web technology. 20 May 2012, webphysics.iupui.edu/jitt/jitt.html.

Ramsden, P. (1992): Learning to Teach in Higher Education. London: Routledge.

Renc-Roe, J. (2006): "Motivation as engaged learning. An experienced teacher's view." In: Ulnicane, I./Dryven, K. (eds): How to Motivate and How to Supervise Students. Budapest: epsnet, pp. 35-45.

4. Motivating Students to Read: Blogs in Philosophy Teaching

Katarína Hrnčiarová, University of Pavol Jozef Šafárik in Košice

4.1 Introduction

This paper aims to introduce the outcomes of an innovation project, which was conducted during the winter semester of 2011. The project concerned a specific issue that is a major problem for the whole department of philosophy: students' insufficient pre-class preparation resulting from not reading the assigned literature. The method applied to solve this problem involved technology based learning: *blog assignments* were introduced to motivate students to read before seminars. The outcomes of this motivation project were evaluated using a questionnaire that elicited basic feedback from students.

The innovated course Philosophy of Language aims to introduce the main philosophical schools or groups of contemporary philosophy and their theoretical approaches in the history of philosophy concerning the problem of language. Moreover, it aims to develop students' capacity of higher level thinking skills such as analytical skills, problem solving skills, the ability to synthesize and integrate information and ideas, the ability to think holistically, the ability to distinguish between fact and opinion, etc. Philosophy of Language is an optional course offered to students who major in Philosophy during the second year of their MA studies. The course is divided into one lecture and one seminar per week. The lecture is taught by an experienced lecturer and the seminar is taught by a doctoral student. During the last semester, ten students attended the course.

The innovation was based on the idea of Kvasz (2005: 21) appealed on teachers to overcome the barriers of stereotypes at students. The innovation project tried to overcome one stereotypical requirement of philosophy seminars, in particular that students are supposed to read a text at home after which the teacher will ask them *factual questions* to answer based on their assigned reading. It was expected that this stereotype can be overcome through the use of opinion questions, which are answered in students' blogs. It was assumed that this method would show students that the text they read can enrich their perspective on the topic and help them to prove or confute their own opinions.

4.2 Aims of the Innovation and Theoretical Background

As it was stated before, the innovation project endeavours to solve the basic problem of students not completing assigned readings before seminars, which results in impossibility of discussing or analysing the text in class. The availability of readings could not be the source of the problem because all materials for seminars were provided at the beginning of semester. The readings were not unbearably long and they were covered during seminars. Therefore, the major problem was how to motivate students to read.

The theoretical background of the innovation project was based on the article by Kvasz (2005). The author discusses three kinds of motivation that can be applied – *external, internal and cognitive.* External motivation is aimed to overcome stereotypes and bring fun to the lecture. Internal motivation is supposed to demonstrate that the topic is interesting by itself or internally. Cognitive motivation should provoke students and stimulate intellectual conflict, prompting students to rethink their attitude or opinion. All three levels of motivation were included in the innovation through the implementation of methods that embodied the various levels. Through the innovation project, this approach was applied to the new class design.

At the level of external motivation students were asked whether they could imagine a class where neither they nor the teacher would speak. Language is such a critical part of our culture in that it facilitates most communication and information transfer. Therefore, this exercise could motivate students to understand language from a philosophical and not only linguistic point of view.

At the level of internal motivation, the chosen method was a student blog. Blog is a web site where students upload their personal journals or short essays on the assigned topic from their reading. Students were assigned to write a short article in the form of a blog (around 400-500 words) that had to be uploaded at least 24 hours before seminars. These continuous tasks were designed to motivate students to read prior to class, to improve students' academic writing skills and also to develop their creativity. By writing a blog, students were also expected to explore the topic, possibly increasing their internal interest in the subject.

At the level of cognitive motivation, the same method was applied. The blog was chosen as a form of cognitive motivation because it provided an opportunity for confrontation, which could make students change their ideas, opinions and attitudes. Students were assumed to become confronted by their classmates about their opinions and therefore motivated to read by the pressure of their study group. The teacher planned to undertake the role of a guide in this case. Since the blog was public, there was also a chance that somebody from outside the class would comment on student ideas. For this reason, it was expected that a shift in students' thinking might occur also as a result of discussion with the public.

Students were therefore motivated to read the assigned texts by the use of *technology-enhanced learning* (TEL), which involves learning through technology outside of the class environment. The particular TEL tool used in this innovation project was the blog.

Blogs, or to be precise weblogs, have been implemented into curricula in different countries. Many articles describe so-called *blended classes*, which consist of web assignments and learning as well as usual face-to-face lectures and seminars. According to the majority of research projects, blended teaching offers more advantages than disadvantages. The following webpage was used to apply blogs as a TEL tool: www.blogger.com. Students were briefly advised how the tool worked during the first seminar class. There were no problems with technology reported by students at that time.

Dziuban, Moskal and Hartman (2005: 5) include several advantages of blended learning. For example: "An additional benefit often reported in blended classes is an increase in interaction over what students and faculty typically perceive in face-to-face courses." This advantage could have been applied to philosophy teaching via blogs as well since students did not need to review word by word the materials or texts given to them during the classes. Instead, only main ideas were stressed, and only the main philosophical problem and its solutions were discussed in the class. Students did not have to repeat the content of the text, but they were free to express their opinions on the problem.

More benefits of the use of blogs in higher education are listed by Mora and Espinosa (2007: 4-5). Even though advantages and benefits prevail (including higher level thinking and connection between students with diverse opinions), Mora and Espinosa (2007: 6) also list several barriers (e.g. Security concerns or software installation). However, those barriers did not exist in this innovation project because of the design of the blog webpage. For instance, blogs were secure because the content of the blogs was not fully public if the student did not want it to be. Also software did not need to be installed and no advertisements were provided by the site itself.

4.3 Research Design

Two types of research designs were applied to evaluate the innovation project. At the beginning, a descriptive design was used to answer the questions of who, what, when, where and how in connection to the innovation problem. This was done through observing the natural class environment, especially how students were influenced by the innovation.

The model of case studies was applied as the second type of research design. Case studies contain in-depth research of a particular problem; in this case the problem was how to motivate one group of students to read the assigned articles. Case studies were applied and discussed in the class environment. For example students were asked to name and explain a case when a speech act can change a reality without any other action, such as the vow during a wedding ceremony.

The main research instrument used to evaluate this innovation project was a questionnaire. Its purpose was to test whether the innovation model had been successfully applied to the natural class environment. The questionnaire was created for the purpose of the one-year program *Inquiry into Student Learning* and it represented a general questionnaire for students of all participants. Questions and answers of students are illustrated in the graph below.

Lastly, the success of the innovation was also evaluated by documentary evidence as well, i.e. Student blogs.

4.4 Findings

It was observed that as a result of the course innovation, seminars became more interactive and maintained progress. Since students were motivated by blog assignments to read texts before the class, their participation increased – they started to talk more often during the class, and there was time to interpret texts critically because time was not used at the beginning of class to review the text content. Students were keen to write blogs from the beginning and during the semester all the blogs were handed in on time.

Data were collected during the last week of the semester by means of the questionnaire. 8 out of 10 students completed the questionnaire. The results are displayed in the form of a stacked bar graph, which represents multiple categories in one single graph (see Figure 5).

The following conclusions resulted from the graph. Questions 14 and 29 offered a picture about student motivation. Answers to question 14 suggested that the course was generally attractive for students. Answers to question 29 about enthusiasm to study implied that half of the participants were enthusiastic, 25% neutral and 25% did not experience any enthusiasm while studying.

Questions 17, 18, and 32 were concerned with the difference between facts and opinions. Students' answers differed as described by the following: while 75% agreed or completely agreed that questions asked during the class were only factual, 75% also claimed (disagreed and completely disagreed) the teacher did not only test their memory. The majority of students (5 out of 8,

Figure 5: Results displayed by questionnaire item.

Source: own depiction

which represent 62.5% of students in the class) expressed in question 32 that not only memory was needed to complete the course. This discrepancy suggests that students are not familiar with the difference between facts and opinions and also that they do not distinguish between memorizing and other thinking skills.

Among other questions concerning student abilities (including questions 21, 22, 24, 25, 30) question 30 was found the most important. It asked students about their analytical skills. Seven students (which represents 87.5% of students in the class) agreed that the course helped them to improve their analytical skills, which was the most important learning objective of the course.

Moreover, according to seven students, the course improved their written communication (measured by question 28). Additionally question 33 concerned information technologies (IT), where 75% of students completely agreed or agreed with the statement that when the use of IT was implemented into the course, it helped their learning, whereas only two students (25%) remained neutral.

Aside from this, two students in their emails expressed appreciation of the innovative course design because using a blog they finally found a place to express their ideas. The innovation was aimed to improve higher level thinking skills at students and most of their blog entries documented this. Students' ability to synthesize and integrate information and ideas increased because at the beginning most of their short essays were informational, but toward the end of the semester, their own opinions were expressed much more frequently. The fulfilment of the learning objectives of the course increased in quality during the semester, such as the analysis of the basic approaches of a philosopher and its comparison with other traditions, the analysis of the argumentative structure of a text, critical thinking of a problem (blog assignment), etc.

4.5 Limitation of the Study and Suggestions for Future Improvement

Several articles listed in the bibliography include research on how weblogs have been successfully implemented in higher education courses. The majority of them prefer blended courses to face-to-face classes. For example, Williams and Jacobs (2004: 235-240) describe into detailed a research project that can be inspiring for further course planning. Also their question-naire included many details that might improve this innovation during the next semester – for example, it could ask whether students consider blogs to be a medium for reflection and what the main reasons are why students do not like to participate in blog-based classes. A similar questionnaire might be implemented into the course in the future.

From the beginning of this innovation project, students had problems in distinguishing between a fact and an opinion. As a result, a discussion about this issue should be included into the introductory seminar next year. This seminar should also include information about annotations and blog design to clarify some possible problematic areas.

At the end of the semester, one additional problem appeared. This problem was related to the condition that doctoral students in Slovakia cannot teach and become responsible for whole courses; they can lead seminars, but not lectures, and they cannot be responsible assessing their students. Despite the effort students brought into their blogs and class participation, their final assessment consisted only of the final test grade. Students did not complain because nine students received the highest grade (A) and only one student got a B. However, the assessment according to their work in the seminars would be completely different: four students would receive a C, four students t a B and only two students an A. The decision not to consider those blog assignments as part of the assessment was surprising. It led to a question that is difficult to answer: Is there a possibility for an innovation of the course when the seminar leader cannot contribute to the final assessment of students?

4.6 Conclusion

This paper aimed to introduce the innovation project based on technology enhanced learning. During the course called Philosophy of Language, blog assignments were implemented to solve the problem of students not reading the assigned texts for seminars. This course illustrated a pervasive problem of the Department of Philosophy – even last year's MA students were refusing to read. If students do not complete the assigned readings for seminars, the main purpose – to teach students to think critically and analytically and to be able to argue for their own opinion – is lost. Therefore the blogs were applied to motivate students to accomplish this goal and improve the quality of seminars for which their texts were assigned.

Blog assignments increased motivation in students to read texts and become aware of their content. In this case, this innovation project was found to be successful. Even though some problems appeared during its application, it can be concluded that the innovation was interesting for students and, after several small changes, it can be applied next term again.

References

Dziuban, C./Moskal, P./Hartman, J. (2005): "Higher education, blended learning and the generations: knowledge is power no more." In: Bourne, J./Moore J. C. (eds.): Elements of quality online education Engaging communities. Needham, MA: Sloan Centre for Education, pp. 1-17.

Kvasz, L. (2005): "On possible approaches to motivation." In: Gregušová, G. (eds.): How to Teach Political Science? The Experience of First-time University Teachers. Budapest: epsnet, pp. 21-26.

Lujan-Mora, S./de Juana-Espinosa, S. (2007): "The use of weblogs in higher education: benefits and barriers." In: Proceedings of the International Technology, Education and Development Conference. 15 April 2012 http://gplsi.dlsi.ua.es/proyectos/webeso/pdf/inted07.pdf.

Williams, J. B./Jacobs, J. (2004): "Exploring the use of blogs as learning spaces in the higher education sector." Australasian Journal of Educational Technology 20, 2, pp. 232-247.

Section 2: Teaching Large Classes

5. Using Blended Learning to Develop Students' Skills and Motivation

Petra Muráriková, Constantine the Philosopher University in Nitra

5.1 Introduction

This paper discusses the challenges of an innovative Bachelor Thesis Seminar, which is a mandatory course for students of Ethics. In order to overcome the problem of (a) weak student motivation for writing their bachelor theses and (b) their lack of academic writing skills, the blended learning approach was chosen to serve this dual purpose. The results of the innovation, as measured by questionnaires, brought unexpected results: although the blended learning created sufficient possibilities for writing skills development, its e-learning element, which aimed to increase students' motivation for writing the bachelor thesis, did not meet this original expectation.

The Bachelor Thesis Seminar aims to provide theoretical as well as practical support for students in the third and final year of their bachelor study program preparing to write their final thesis. Throughout the course, emphasis should be put on the introduction of formal criteria of bachelor thesis writing, and, at the same time, attention should be paid to concrete steps in the preparation of each thesis.

Due to various reasons, however, this general aim usually failed in numerous aspects. The course, having a form either of weekly sessions or of a single block of sessions at the end of winter semester (consisting of approximately eight classes taught during one day), did not lead to desired outcomes. The weekly session format consisted solely of discussions or consultations of the problems and needs of students; however, as no concrete outcome of student activity was expected or evaluated, most students made little or no progress in writing their thesis. The block format, on the other hand, offered at least some more systematic introduction to bachelor thesis writing, but still failed in giving students enough opportunities for advancing thinking about their research and for practicing academic writing. What is more, taking place at the end of winter semester, this support came too late.

Both formats resulted in students' procrastination in writing the bachelor thesis. For this reason, many students did not make systematic progress on their thesis until a month or two before the final deadline. Moreover, because of the large number of students at the Department of Ethics, the supervisors struggled with being supportive enough to their students throughout the time of thesis preparation, particularly when they were under pressure of other responsibilities. As a consequence, students' needs were at times at variance with supervisors' actual capacities for help, which was manifested in the quality of theses.

Probably as a result of this, students often perceived writing the bachelor thesis as a kind of "inevitable evil", being unable to think about it in a positive, broader perspective. In other words, students were very often ill-prepared and unmotivated to write their theses. Consequently, a course leading to this "obligation" was rarely welcomed with enthusiasm and interest. In connection to this rather passive and disdainful attitude, the large number of students (35), each lacking motivation and demanding a high input of skills, was considered to be the core of the teaching challenge.

5.2 Aims of the Innovation and Theoretical Background

The innovation therefore aimed to create several opportunities for a group of thirty-five students to start to think about and work on their theses during the winter semester, rather than in the middle of summer semester. This aim included thinking about the purpose of their thesis, its aims, research methodology, etc., but also, equally importantly, thinking about the purpose of writing a thesis as such in a broader perspective. The nature of the innovation was conditioned by both the department policy, which allows teaching staff a great deal of freedom in matters of course curriculum and teaching process, and my convenient personal timetable as the course leader.

Drawing on these two main advantages, the principle of *blended learning* was chosen to stand at the heart of the innovation. Blended learning may be described as a type of learning which combines traditional face-to-face classroom methods with computer-mediated activities. As Garrison and Kanuka (2004: 5) point out, blended learning is not only about finding the right mix of technologies or increasing access to learning. Rather, it represents a fundamental reconceptualization and reorganization of the teaching and learning dynamic (Garrison and Kanuka 2004: 3).

Keeping the identified teaching problems in mind, the blended learning model seemed to offer a strategy to cope with both pedagogic challenges.

42

Above all, the model was expected to contribute to the aim of creating possibilities for students to start working systematically on the bachelor thesis in winter semester. Furthermore, besides creating plenty of possibilities for academic writing skills development, the expected asset was grounded in the virtual part of the blended learning model. Taking various e-learning advantages into consideration (space and time flexibility, possibility for self-paced learning, reduced number of personal meetings, etc.) The virtual learning environment seemed to be a promising tool for increasing student motivation. This expectation was based on Garrison and Kanuka's (2004: 4) claim that asynchronous computer-mediated activities support critical thinking, writing skills and, most importantly in the present context, motivation, among other things.

To address the problems, Middendorf and Pace's (2004: 3) *Model of Seven Steps to Overcome Obstacles to Learning* was applied. The authors recommend following steps:

1. Define a bottleneck to students' learning;
2. Think of what should be done in order to get past this bottleneck;
3. Consider how students can be shown how to get past the bottleneck;
4. Create opportunities for practice and offer feedback to students;
5. Use different ways of motivating students to continue through the process;
6. Check whether students have mastered the operations at the end of the process;
7. Share the resulting knowledge about learning with others.

Applying this model, it was realized that the bottleneck to students' learning laid in the lack of their skills and motivation. The answer to the question of how to get past this bottleneck was found in proper instructions and opportunities for practice; the lack of motivation was resolved by constructing several motivational stimuli. As far as skills development was concerned, the third step was realized by introducing the practical steps in gaining these skills throughout the course. The motivation development was carried out by an e-assignment called "I Study Ethics: Reflexive Paper."

Sequentially, to create opportunities for practice and offering feedback, the course content was redesigned and a virtual classroom was set up. The last but one step mainly entailed creating the rules and assessment part of the course. In order to evaluate the success of the innovation both for individual course elements and overall, measurement tools were also prepared in the sixth step. Finally, the last step, which relates to sharing gained experience with others, is hopefully being carried out by this chapter. Applying this model into the course, blended learning seemed to be an appropriate solution, especially for steps 4-6 of the stated model, in which motivation and personal feedback were discussed.

The reorganization and redesign of the teaching and learning dynamic was based on the rotation of two formats of teaching: in-class and e-learning. In practice, the group of 35 students was divided into two sub-groups (A, B) which alternated in the two main formats and learning environments every week. Two exceptions within the in-class format (in terms of teaching environments) were introduced: while the majority of in-class sessions took place in a classroom setting, one session took place in a café and another in a computer room. This way, four learning environments were blended: classroom, virtual classroom, café, and computer room. The impact of each of these could have been analysed in detail. However, within this report, only the two main (and most typical) learning environments, classroom and virtual classroom, will be discussed.

5.3 Research Design

The effect of the innovation as a whole was evaluated in two main areas of "educational" and "motivational" goals. The achievement of the "educational" goal was measured by regular weekly e-assignments and a final compulsory non-standardized e-questionnaire at the end of the semester. This final evaluation questionnaire consisted of 35 questions, 11 of which were open-ended. The remaining closed-ended questions were based on four or five-point Likert-type scales mostly to measure the degree of agreement or disagreement with the given statement. The response rate was 100%.

The achievement of the "motivational" goal was measured in several steps. Firstly, the assignment for the second session, called "I Study Ethics: Reflexive Paper," functioned as a "point of departure" as questions about motivation for, and satisfaction with the chosen study program arose. Secondly, the third session, taking place in a café to stimulate students' motivation, was followed by a "Café workshop questionnaire." This feedback questionnaire consisted of 13 questions, ten of which were based on scales and the remaining open-ended. Having been an assignment, the questionnaire was compulsory for all of the course participants but obviously not assessed.

Thirdly, a "Bachelor thesis: reflexive paper" in the middle of the semester questioned the problem of how students perceived the writing of the bachelor thesis in a broader perspective. Lastly, the final evaluation questionnaire designed to measure the educational goal achievement also dealt with questions of increasing motivation. Although a qualitative interpretation of the students' reflexive papers, using the method of document analysis, could be a great contribution to the analysis of innovation effects, for the purpose of this paper, the relevant responses from the final questionnaire have mainly been used.

Being non-standardized questionnaires, however, both the café feedback questionnaire and the final evaluation questionnaire had their weak points, mainly of a dual nature. Firstly, some of the open-ended questions, for example the question *"Would you prefer to use virtual and in-class format combined or only in-class work?"* Could have worked more effectively as a scale-based closed-ended question. Secondly, the results revealed that some open-ended questions and scales (and for that reason also the responses) were equivocal in their nature. For example, for the item *"Define the state of development of your bachelor thesis before taking the course"*, the option *"I have been thinking about it a lot"* was not clear enough, as it could not be judged whether the student thought about the content of the thesis, or about the duty of writing it. Adding more specific formulations or more explanative sub-questions could have improved the weaknesses of the last point mentioned.

5.4 Findings

5.4.1 Educational Goal

In order to provide an analysis of the results and findings, each aim will be presented separately. The purpose of the educational aim, as stated above, was to create several opportunities for students to start thinking about and working on their theses early on. Because the data concerning students' stage of development of their bachelor theses before taking the course is (as stated in an example above) open to many interpretations and purveys almost no reliable propositions, only the final results will be presented, which unfortunately precludes the possibility of seeing a clear progress line.

Keeping the first of the aims in mind, two items of the final evaluation questionnaire directly reveal its achievement. First of all, 44% of students somewhat agreed and 50% completely agreed with the statement *"Throughout the course I started to think more intensively about the content of my bachelor thesis"*. Only two students (6%) somewhat disagreed with this statement. However trivial this aim may appear at first sight, the matter itself is just not that simple.

In fact, personal attendance at regular sessions without substantial student engagement does not necessarily lead to the desired effect. The point behind this is that active thinking about the subject does not come automatically as a result of attending the course. The level of active involvement of students' minds depends on various circumstances, among others, on stimulating inputs of teaching approach. Therefore, it was necessary to document whether students were not only physically present in the classroom, but above all, the result of their participation in the course.

The second part of the educational goal was aimed at starting to work on the bachelor thesis within the span of the course. To document the attainment of this aim, the respondents were asked to express their dis/agreement with the statement "*I have started to collect information required to commence writing the bachelor thesis*". The results showed that 35% somewhat agreed and 62% completely agreed with this statement. Only one person (3%) somewhat disagreed. Even though it may seem unclear what "collecting information" implies, this type of obscurity disappears on the basis of familiarization with the topics students went over.

The question stemming from these results is that of the extent to which the innovation, being based on blended learning, contributed to this outcome. The preponderance of tasks which could lead to the stated goal was mainly grounded in the e-learning part of the innovation. Three items of the final evaluation questionnaire focused on its influence on goal achievement. The results showed that half of the students (50%) somewhat agreed and 44% completely agreed that "*online assignments helped them to think about their bachelor thesis*". Similarly, 56% somewhat agreed and 26% completely agreed that "*online tasks and reading assignments stimulated the process/initiation of writing my bachelor thesis*". To conclude, 47% somewhat agreed and 39% completely agreed that "*regular assignments helped them start to work on their bachelor thesis*".

Quite apparently, the e-learning part of the teaching contributed rather significantly to the achievement of the "educational" goal. Accordingly, the in-class teaching format, enriched with e-learning potential, created a productive space for reaching the stated aim.

5.4.2 Motivational Goal

To evaluate the achievement of the other, so-called "motivational" goal, the item directly measuring its impact is represented by the statement "*The course motivated me to work on my bachelor thesis*". The majority of students responded they somewhat (47%) or completely (44%) agreed with the statement, while two students (6%) somewhat disagreed and one person (3%) disagreed completely. These results, being more positive than negative, may also be supported by responses to open-ended questions in which students often expressed their appreciation of individual feedback, invested time from their teacher, the variation of activities and tasks at the in-class format sessions, the responsible attitude of teacher, the relaxed atmosphere, etc. Students considered these to be stimulating and motivating.

Likewise with the previous goal, it is necessary to clarify to what extent the innovation contributed to such results. To start with, most of the students (77%) would prefer blended learning (a combination of in-class and e-learning formats), while seven students (21%) would choose an in-class-only format. These results show the combination of both formats was appreciated but does not in fact prove that the innovation as such contributed to students' increased motivation to write the bachelor thesis. As e-learning was the new element in the innovation itself, it had been expected that it would also carry the highest motivational potential.

The results of the final evaluation questionnaire, however, documented an almost opposite effect. The request to order learning environments according to personal preference showed that only three people (9%) ranked the virtual environment first, and at the same time, the virtual learning environment achieved last place (38%) in this ordering. The most preferred learning environment was the café in which one session took place (50%). The reasons for this choice are understandable: the change of the place and relaxed atmosphere stimulated the interest and motivation of the students. Surprisingly enough, the second most preferred learning environment was the classroom (44%), with just two votes separating it from the café as the most preferred learning environment.

Moreover, these findings are also confirmed by the last analysed questionnaire item, "*Which of the learning environments motivated you the most?*" The preponderance of respondents (44%) were most motivated by the classroom learning environment, 38% chose the café, 9% were for the computer room and for the same number of students, three (9%), the virtual environment was the most motivating one.

Several interpretations of such surprising results for e-learning can be made. Firstly, the fact that the students had never had an experience with e-learning before could have affected their perceptions of the way of learning in more disruptive than productive way. Secondly, the lack of experience with a virtual learning environment may imply a lack of skills. In fact, many of the students admitted they had been having problems with computer literacy at the beginning of the course. Thirdly, the students' idea of the virtual learning environment could be directly associated with the weekly assignments transmitted through this medium. The amount of workload, even though admitted by the majority of students to be useful, could have diminished the enthusiasm, and in this way influenced the motivational potential of the virtual learning environment.

Although all these interpretations may be of significance in the results, at least one more will be discussed below. Drawing on the student comments from the questionnaire, students' frequent substantiation for their preference of classroom as the most motivational learning environment was grounded in the argument of personal contact with the teacher. Correspondingly, one of the findings of this innovation is that face-to-face contact, personal feedback, individual encouragement, immediate response to one's needs and many other positives of classroom learning environment still have great motivational potential.

A certain loss of the "personal" in the age of modern technologies is inevitable, but at the same time, the demands of modernity cannot overshadow the necessity for vital personal interactions and relationships. The results document that the innovations based on low input of personal stimuli may be reduced in their motivational potential. In other words, face-to-face interactions seem to possess stronger motivational potential than interactions based on a non-personal basis (despite being enriched by regular individualized, personal e-communication with students).

This is not, however, to condemn e-learning as a way of learning deprived first of personal stimuli and then of motivational potential. In fact, e-learning, once providing individual feedback might become more stimulating than personal contact. Unfortunately, e-learning is sometimes used not only to allow for distance between teacher and student for practical reasons, but also as a tool for teachers for avoiding labour-intensive personal interaction with students.

To prevent this, teachers using e-learning should be aware of students' need for personal (even though not always face-to-face) interactions and their potential for achievement of common goals. Regular contact, the teachers' interest, their (online) accessibility, as well as their positive attitude towards this way of teaching at the end verify their level of student-centeredness. The above mentioned characteristics of successful use of e-learning ensure also the elimination of its negative effects in the form of students' feelings of isolation and their loss of motivation.

5.5 Limitations of the Study and Suggestions for Future Improvement

The number of possible interpretations of the results clearly draws the area for improvement. Reworked measurement tools would therefore be a challenge for future teachers of this course. The other area for course improveement would be the management of time, effort and interest on the part of the teacher.

The initial willingness to offer a high level of various inputs to the design of this course and especially to its students required heavy time and energy investments. The assessment of regular e-assignments was based on individual feedback offering a list of strengths, gently indicated weaknesses, suggestions, recommendations and encouragements. The feedback on the tasks within classroom sessions did not, however, fall behind that of the virtual sessions. The appreciation of each student's work; proper rectification and regulation; an emphatic attitude to students' limits and previous skills and, at the same time, motivating assignments; control not only of verbal but also non-verbal communication; all of these demands involved a high degree of concentration. The result was often a struggle between (from time to time) idealistic goals and actual capacities (personal and physical).

The "trap" behind such an approach is that once teachers start to put themselves into teaching as described above, they are "bound" by the heightened expectations of their students. Nevertheless, the reason not to abandon such an exhausting approach lies in seeing the fruit it brings. Students' progress, increased interest, feedback, and willingness to cooperate and actively participate is both fulfilling and motivating.

After all, the comments from the final evaluation questionnaire such as "*I appreciate you both as a teacher and as a person...*", "*... you are my great motivation...*", "*...your words like super, ok or take it easy were moving me forward...*", "*... carry on with your attitude, it is great!*", "*I am thankful you were willing to devote so much time to us...*", "*...this course was a great asset for me...*" and many others demonstrated a kind of emotional satisfaction, creating the feeling that it is worthwhile to sacrifice a lot in order to see the results. Above all, it was the anticipation of long-term consequences of teaching and the awareness of the moral nature of the teaching profession that resulted in the feeling of responsibility for taking advantage of the chance to stand so close to the point from which a student's life can take a different, more valuable course.

Apart from this, the Bachelor Thesis Seminar is a very special type of course, with a potential for both professional and personal development. No other course within the study programs at the Department of Ethics opens a space for such intensive personal interactions with students. If a more efficient approach from teacher's part was desired, ignoring all the arguments above and having other reasons for doing so (e.g. Other courses and duties), there are several suggestions to be taken into consideration.

Firstly, a reduced workload of e-assignments would definitely ease the amount of time devoted to reviewing them. What to leave and what to skip should, however, be decided upon an analysis of the student group's needs. Secondly, in the case of hand-in tasks sharing the same set of student mistakes, collective feedback might be a time-saving solution. In this instance, there are two acceptable ways of its distribution: either a frontal presentation at the session (also requiring preparation and presentation time) or a peer-assessment (with the risk of time consumption devoted to teaching students how to perform it).

A third suggestion might be that of a structured individual feedback in written form, similar to the approach that was chosen, though differing in the feedback formulation. A set of structures used for assessment of common positives and negatives can be formed in advance, and the teacher can therefore react to each assignment promptly, without spending a lot of time formulating his or her ideas into full sentences. These structures (strengths, weaknesses, recommendations, and encouragements), in the form of a grading rubric, can serve as individualized assessment, according to the needs of each student. Finally, teaching the course for a second or third time would result in more fine-tuned and efficient approach.

5.6 Conclusion

This report summarizes experiences with teaching innovation of mandatory course Bachelor Thesis Seminar. Its aim was to provide theoretical as well as practical support for students in the final year of their bachelor study program.

The necessity to innovate the teaching approach was grounded in the importance of starting to work on the bachelor thesis early on. In order to solve this, two sub-problems were identified: students' lack of skills relating to the preparation and writing of the thesis and a lack of motivation for doing so. To address these problems, the model of blended learning was chosen. This way, sufficient opportunities for students' skills development were created. At the same time, students' motivation was expected to get increased, having the possibility of taking advantage of blended learning's virtual element (space and time flexibility, possibility for self-paced learning, reduced number of personal meetings, etc.). The effects of the innovation were measured by two compulsory non-standardized e-questionnaires.

To sum up the results and findings, the innovation in the form of blended learning proved to be useful for achieving the "educational", and partially the "motivational" goal. Blended learning, being a combination of in-class and virtual learning environments, created opportunities for structured progression and prevented students form procrastinating in writing their bachelor theses. Blended learning was welcomed as a learning environment by most students; however, it was not the e-learning that students appreciated as motivating but rather the classroom meetings. In fact, the final evaluation questionnaire revealed that e-learning was the least preferred learning environment, as far as the motivation was concerned.

Nevertheless, this can be considered rather a question of expectations than of results. What is more, students' preference of the classroom setting might well be a secondary effect of the introduction of the e-learning setting (e.g. The more relaxed pace of learning in the classroom may have been caused by the transfer of tasks and assignments to the e-learning environment). Verification of these conjectures would require further examination.

Despite the fact that e-learning, as part of the blended learning approach, did not fulfil the original expectations about its attractiveness and motivational stimulus for students, the innovation succeeded in accomplishing both main aims stated above. In accordance with evidence (Garrison and Kanuka 2004: 6) about the potential of blended learning (as such) to become more effective in comparison to the traditional classroom model, the course confirmed the advantages commonly attributed to the blended learning approach, including space and time flexibility, the possibility for self-paced learning, and a reduced number of personal meetings.

References

Pace, D./Middendorf, J. (2004): "Decoding the disciplines: Helping students learn disciplinary ways of thinking." New Directions in Teaching and Learning 98, pp. 1-12.

Garrison, D. R./Kanuka, H. (2004): 'Blended learning: Uncovering its transformative potential in higher education.' The Internet and Higher Education 7, pp. 95-105.

6. Problem Solving Class as a Tool for Effective Large Group Teaching

Peter Dzurjaník, University of Constantine the Philosopher in Nitra

6.1 Introduction

The aim of this paper is to present the results of the teaching innovation the purpose of which was to find ways to work with large-group classes, to keep students focused and to encourage more participation.

In the fall of 2011, I taught for the first time the course entitled The Pillars of the European Civilization, which was attended by 86 students. The design of the course was my responsibility with the course being something between a lecture and seminar. The purpose of this course was to provide students from various departments of the faculty with basic knowledge about the history and development of European culture and civilization. There were not only freshmen enrolled in this course, but more advanced students, too.

With this number of students, it is usually very difficult to give everyone feedback concerning their individual knowledge, understanding and application of what they had learned. While teaching courses with similar number of students in the past, student strategy to pass the course included above all studying intensively at home shortly before the test at the end of the semester. Obviously, this strategy did not work as many of them failed to understand questions on the test and the proportion of students failing the exam was high (nearly half of the class). Moreover, there was another problem related to teaching such a large group of students. Many of them hid in the anonymity of the big group and remained silent during class, or worse, disturbed others. Classes automatically shifted from seminars to lectures at one point during the semester due to the high number of students, the difficulties in making them cooperate, and the poor standard of their works. I had to prepare notes for the students, and later our sessions became regular lectures.

The last important factor influencing the teaching was time at which the class was held on Tuesday from 6.15 to 7.45 PM. Tuesday is regularly the day when students – especially freshmen – have the most classes of the week. Therefore, students were coming to class very tired, had problems staying focused, and did not want to participate during class.

The chosen way to deal with the described challenge was to divide students into smaller groups and use the method of *problem solving groups*. This method included assigning open-ended questions related to the topic of the class to groups of students. Students' role was to answer these questions with the help and advice of the teacher. The whole class then discussed these responses.

6.2 Aims of the Innovation and Theoretical Background

Regarding the main teaching problem, i.e. Large group teaching, the aims of the innovation were as follows:

a) Find a way for students to participate and cooperate with their colleagues;
b) Reduce the time that students are unfocused and prevent situations of disruption;
c) Create a communicating class where everybody, including the teacher, could exchange opinions and information.

The strategy to overcome this teaching problem was based on the paper of Cohen (2008). Cohen described similar problems with students' motivation and focus and described the kinds of methods he had used to make students more active in the class and participate more in what was going on during the session. Cohen's starting point was a poll, where he asked students why they thought the activity in class was important. After some traditional responses (it helps increase the attention of students, the class is more interesting) he got another answer: the teacher can use students' activity as a tool to assess whether students understand the subject matter properly and whether they have been focusing on important parts of curriculum (Cohen 2008: 609).

Cohen came to realize that evaluation and assessment do not only consist of tests and quizzes. Students' activity can be used as feedback on what and how they are learning, if they understand the issue correctly, and the way they think. This gives the teacher more space to respond immediately during the class and not after the test results. At the same time this assessment is not just about giving a grade to students, but rather about supporting the learning process.

This experience made Cohen (2008: 612) .make a list of four recommendations about what teachers should do to encourage group activity and how to assess it:

1. Divide large groups into smaller ones and give students small problems addressing issues of the topic for which several correct answers exist;
2. Encourage students to ask questions. They should be provoking and encourage discussion;
3. Give the students short written tasks (e.g. A task to summarize today's class in three sentences);
4. Include some short presentations of students

These steps should result in the teacher always having responses from students during the class and he or she can adjust their teaching immediately. Students can assess themselves too, right on the spot. They can find out where the black or grey areas of their understanding are and ask their teacher for clarification; they think more about connections, and they come up with interesting points of view and with other ideas or opinions more often.

For the innovated course, the first method was chosen. It was believed that the best way to teach a class with many students might be to divide them into problem solving groups. It was considered probably the only way to work with them efficiently. The next step was to assess students according to their in-class activity. But the most important principle was to create accurate and clear rules for how students could achieve points for their activity and then to present these rules to the students in the first session and include them in the syllabus.

The other three elements suggested by Cohen were present, too. After their work in a session, the group leaders presented the results of assigned problems. Students always knew that they could ask any question related to the topic or bring up some other topics to discuss. The third suggestion (the short written task) was used only twice.

Personal talks with students who had already taken this course with another teacher were very helpful, too. I was told what they liked from her sessions, what they would change, or what they missed.

The original plan was to have every odd (first, third, fifth, etc.) Session contain problem solving work in small groups. About one third of the class time was spent lecturing, the second third was reserved for problem solving, and the last third for discussion between groups and for class revision to find out what was unclear or misunderstood. Every person in the group had his or her role (an organizer, a record-keeper, a presenter and others' role was to think about the problem). These roles were rotated during the semester, so every student tried every role. No matter the role, every student in the group had to summarize in written form the problem they were solving and the outcomes. The group members did not change, so students stayed in the same group from the beginning to the end. Their work was rewarded with additional points for activity in their groups.

Every even session had a different design bringing some new aspects of interaction, for example student presentations, teacher presentations, role-play, etc.

6.3 Research Design

In order to evaluate the results of this innovation, data was collected at the beginning, during, and at the end of the semester. The aim of collecting data at the beginning and throughout the semester was to learn about students' expectations from the course, what preferences, motivation and needs they had and what their opinions were on participating in class. Students were asked to respond to an anonymous questionnaire and some were asked to provide their opinion in an interview. Additionally, tests scores in the middle of the semester were used as another source of information about the outcomes of the innovation.

Using the questionnaire, it was possible to adjust the course to students' expectations and needs, which was a way to encourage more active and willing participation during sessions. Individual talks with students were similar to the questionnaire. Some students were asked in their free time about their opinions on working in groups, if they had experiences with working in teams and what expectations they had. The main advantage of the personal talks over the questionnaire was the ability to react to answers and ask additional questions that were not included in the questionnaire.

The innovation of teaching was based on dividing students into smaller groups to solve problems related to the topic of the session. Not many students had experience with this type of teaching and thus were concerned about how to learn for their tests. Since the test reflected the new style of teaching there was an assumption that if the students were successful in it, they would be more confident and motivated to continue with the innovated way of teaching. Tests enabled students to see if they could use their knowledge in practice and if they were focused on the main aspects and facts in their curriculum, too. The results showed where students misunderstood something, and provided useful feedback on what teacher should improve (what to explain more clearly, which areas can be difficult to understand, etc.).

The teacher's reflection was based on observing the students' behaviour and activity during the sessions. Regarding the test results as another evaluation tool of innovation, there was an important question: Will the students of the class who used methods of team work in small groups and problem solving have better test results compared to the test results in the past? These tests contained the open-ended questions, whose aim was to find connections between learnt facts and their application. The level of test difficulty was the same (approved by the teacher who taught this course before).

The students could achieve 40 points during the semester. A minimum of 25 points were needed to pass the course. There were two tests (each worth 12 points), so to pass the whole course, students still needed to collect certain points from activities, even if they had good test results. The idea of activity points was brought as an encouraging tool for students' cooperation, an increased level of focus during class and as a prevention of disturbance. In each class, students could earn one or two points (or zero if they did not work at all), so at the end of semester they could have earned a total of 16 points for participation. Negative points were not used. In cases when students were unprepared for the lesson or disturbed others, they had to leave the classroom and, of course, were marked as absent. This had better effect than negative points.

If a student was absent for a session, he or she had the opportunity to get missing points by completing short, smaller tasks in the next lesson. It was supposed that this system would be more motivating for students to be active in the class. If students did not wish to get the best grade from the course, they were still motivated to be active – at least to some extent – in order to pass the points limit. Since they did not know how many points they would score in the tests at the end of the semester, they tried to get as many points from activities as they could.

6.4 Findings

The questionnaire from the beginning of the semester revealed that almost none of the students read the syllabus – less than ten people did. So practically none knew how the course would be organized and what the requirements were for passing it.

When questioned on their opinion of student participation in the class, most students responded: it depends on what kind of activity is expected from them. About 70% answered this way. Another 20% said that students were supposed to be active and help to improve their course through questions, ideas and communication between teacher and students. The rest thought that they did not need to be active and they were not used to being passive from high school. Moreover, they were afraid of talking in front of others due to their lack of knowledge. Three or four people wrote that due to the late time of my course it would be very difficult for them to pay attention and to be active after a full day of listening and learning in other teachers'.

Many suggestions given on the questionnaire were about what students liked in the past and what topics were attractive for them. These suggestions were used to adjust the course, to rework the classes and to design problems for groups that would be perceived as more practical by students.

As it was mentioned before, two tests were used (one in the middle and one at the end of the semester). The results of the first test were a positive encouragement for the students. A lot of students scored well on the test. Students realized that their previous work in groups had helped them to learn and remember more as well as to apply their knowledge in practice. From the 84 students completing the first test, 61 students (73%) earned more than 7 points (which is 58% of points) and 42 (50%) students earned 9 points (75% of all points). The average score was 9.3 points from maximum 12 points (78%).

The results from the second test (completed by 86 students) were worse than in the first one (see Figure 6). This was not because the test was more difficult, but because students did not prepare as well as for the first one. The average score was 5.8 points from 12 (48%). The reason is discussed in the fifth section of this article.

Figure 6: Results of the first test in the middle of semester and second at the end of semester (x-axis: scored points; maximum was 12 points in each test, y-axis: number of students).

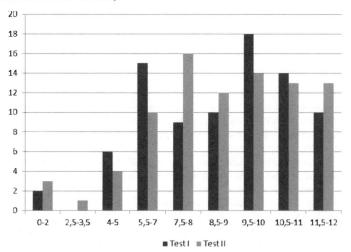

Source: own depiction

In the graph, it is possible to see improvement in the first category – 13 students scored 11.5-12 points. These were students who had really poor results on first test or they had been absent during it and so needed to carefully prepare for the second test in order to score maximum points, if they wanted to pass the exam.

Finally, 7% of all students did not pass the course (FX; 5 people) and 3% (3 people) achieved the best – A grade. 16% (14 people) scored B and 31% (27 students) C and same amount (31%, 27 students) had D. 11% of students got E (9 people). One person had to be classified by paper work, because she could not attend the class due her health condition.

6.5 Limitation of the Study and Suggestions for Future Improvement

As mentioned before, there was an initial idea to differentiate between even and odd sessions. However, students were not used to working in groups and using their findings as material for their studying. So the idea concerning even and odd lessons had to be dropped and the focus was only on the problem solving groups. Using so many other approaches only complicated the situation. Certainly, I was not used to leading this type of teaching, so despite my preparation I had to change my approach.

The second problematic area was the heterogeneous composition of the class. There were students studying different majors and thus with different needs. The ideal solution would be to split all students into two groups (historians and archaeologists – other students) and to have two different courses with different tests for them. But unfortunately, I could not impact this.

The idea of having two tests was basically a good approach. However, when many students achieved very good results in the first test, they found that there was not much of a problem achieving points for in-class activities if they did what they were supposed to do. As a result, they did not feel the need to prepare for the second test – they knew they would need only few points to pass the minimum requirement of 25 points. If they knew that they would need for example 4 points to earn the grade they wished, they answered enough questions for 4 points and then finished and handed out their test. This is what some students said when interviewed informally at the end of semester.

To avoid this situation, the teacher can raise the amount of points needed to pass the course, or decrease the points for the first test and increase the amount of points for the second test. Then students would be motivated to remain active during the whole semester.

In the end, the new teaching method had desired effect: students could pass the test with the knowledge they gained from their work in groups. Moreover, after some five classes, when students got accustomed to this type of teaching they lost their shyness and become involved in the learning process. From their reactions it was evident they enjoyed new way of teaching. The atmosphere was cheerful, full of excited voices and movement. Of course, from time to time things did not go as smoothly as was described for many reasons, for example students seemed really exhausted, or the topic was difficult to understand. I was trying to act only in role of a guide, or a mentor, who encouraged their ideas and helped them to organize their work or to provide them with some information. The students' first success – test results – only supported their willingness to go on.

However, there are still things to improve. For example, I could use presentations from the computer or play movie clips. Additionally, the teacher could better prepare the problems to solve and make them more interesting, and try to adapt to changes in the class, such as atmosphere and speed of work. But now I have some experience and I can build on it. Generally, group work with this amount of students is an optimal way to manage teaching them. I believe I will have more time to prepare my next course, so my work during next semesters should be much easier.

6.6 Conclusion

The course that underwent the innovation was called The Pillars of the European Civilization, which was a course primarily for freshmen of the various departments of the Faculty of Arts. It was a mixture of lectures and seminars. The number of students was 86. The teaching problem included the challenge of how to teach a large group of students, and moreover, how to keep students focused and encourage more participation in the class. Cohen's (2008) ideas served as a source of inspiration for the innovation. It included dividing students into smaller groups and letting them solve problems that did not have simple answers, but rather provided creative spaces for many opinions and possibilities.

Thanks to the innovation, the students understood the issues better and, moreover, were also able to apply their knowledge in practice and make connections. The new form of assessment was created as well where the focus was not only on tests, but on the students' participation in class, too. Points for activities supported their efforts to participate.

The atmosphere in the class was better, too. Discussions after their work helped students to immediately find out what they did not understand or misunderstood. It helped students to work in teams and to present their results to others, too.

Teaching large groups of students this way is considered the most efficient and fruitful way and I plan to stick to it for my next courses. Now I know what areas of ancient history are preferred by students and what kind of problems are more troublesome than useful. Experiences from teaching this course helped the teacher to improve in organizing students' work and to know how to teach the most difficult issues in curriculum in an easier and more understandable way. But one semester is too short to master teaching this way and it will take a longer time to solve and avoid all the possible obstacles.

References

Cohen, M. (2008): "Participation as assessment: Political Science and classroom assessment techniques." PS: Political Science & Politics 41, 3, pp. 609-612.

Section 3: Teaching Courses Rich in Complex Terminology

7. Mnemonics and Creativity as Tools for Enhancing Long-term Knowledge Retention

Adriana Boleková, University of Pavol Jozef Šafárik in Košice

> "Studying is the process that is used to decide
> what to learn and what to remember and recall."
> James. F. Sheperd

7.1 Introduction

The aim of this paper is to report on the results of an innovative intervention and the resulting changes in teaching and student learning. Anatomy, one of the most important courses in a medical doctoral degree program, was chosen as the course to undergo intervention. The basic problem for this course was how to enhance the long-term retention of the most important knowledge. The innovation improved students' memory and imagination using mnemonics and creativity. As I am the Deputy Head of Education in the Anatomy department, it was possible to apply the innovation of the teaching and learning methods with minimal limiting factors. The effect of the innovation was measured by comparing assessment test results of a group of students who were taught in a new way with a group of students who were taught traditionally.

General and Oral Anatomy is a compulsory, two-term course taught in the first year of Dental Medicine. This course consists of three lectures and four practical classes in a dissecting room per week. Approximately 60 students were in the group taught in the Slovak language and 25 students were in the English language group. The number of students in the dissecting room was about ten in each group.

Anatomy should provide students with the basic information about the anatomical relations in the human body, with students having to recognize and name all parts and structures of the human body using the precise

Anatomical nomenclature. Detailed systematic anatomy and topographical relationships of the organs and structures of the head and neck are substantial for dental students; the basic and general knowledge of systematic and topographical anatomy of the human body below head and neck help them to understand the human body entirely.

At our school the main approach to the teaching of anatomy is still very traditional; the main principles of education are the same as they were in the past. It is assumed that the best way to learn the human anatomy is by means of a cadaveric classic dissection supplemented by factual lectures. However, it is also true, that the nature of anatomy education has changed over the past decade due to an enormity of advances in anatomical imaging and teaching and the nature of a new generation of students who are the product of the interactive generation, meaning they learn differently from students of past years. Following the new trends in teaching methods, it is necessary to pay more attention to quality, depth and effectiveness of medical education. The modern tools intended to support the educational process offer possibilities that allow teachers to present their teaching in an effective and more demonstrative way.

Our department has been also trying to make use of new teaching processes with substantial attention to anatomy lectures, by using information and communication technologies in education. Because imagination is a very important aspect in learning anatomy, simulations and virtualization methods are used to revive anatomy education. 3D virtual models serve to help students imagine the anatomical structures like in the real body and to achieve as high precision as they need (Majerník et al. 2011: 4).

7.2 Aims of the Innovation and Theoretical Background

Bloom's taxonomy (Bloom 1956, see Atherton 2011) can be used in anatomy to categorize course goals and assessments into three cognitive objective competences: *knowledge, comprehension* and *application*. The competence knowledge is obtained by observation and recall of information. Questions for students can begin with words such as: list, define, tell, describe, identify, show, label, collect, name, what, where, etc. This competence is the most important in anatomy as the description of organs and their parts is the main content of this subject. The second competence comprehension is demonstrated through an understanding of information by interpreting facts, comparing, contrasting, ordering, or grouping. Students can be asked to practice this competence using phrases as for example: summarize, describe, contrast, associate, distinguish, estimate, differentiate, etc.

The last, but not least of Bloom's competences used in anatomy is application, demonstrated by skills such as: using information, solving problems and using required skills or knowledge. Students can be instructed to apply their knowledge using verbs such as: demonstrate, complete, illustrate, show, solve, classify, etc. Students have to learn description of organs, and they need to understand the relationships between them.

Though three cognitive objective competences are relevant to learning anatomy, only one of the affective objectives from the Bloom's taxonomy is applicable in anatomy: receiving phenomena with awareness, willingness to hear, and selected attention. An example of this in practices is for students to show other students the structures respectfully. Students using new methods can explain their detailed knowledge learned from facts to each other.

The general problem in learning anatomy is that it requires too much memorization of new, often difficult terminology of seemingly complicated anatomical nomenclature. Therefore, it would be beneficial to find out how to improve the long-term retention of General and Oral Anatomy knowledge and how to teach these strategies for students' use in their future clinical practice. This problem pertains to associative learning that leads to accurate reproduction or recall of information.

Biggs differentiates learning into two types: *deep* and *surface learning*. The deep approach (1999: 16) makes knowledge personal and relevant to real-world application. The surface approach to learning (1999: 14) relies on memorization and does not lead to deeper understanding. Both of these types of learning should be used when learning anatomy. Deep learning is important for understanding the problematic details and mutual relations between organs and their structures. Surface learning leads to quick recall of anatomical terms. It is the way how difficult nomenclature can be taught more easily.

However, it is important to point out that no students have bad memory because 'bad memory' is only the result of insufficient attention. Most students have really good memories, but they just do not use them efficiently. Nobody taught students how to use memory. Early repetition of new things is the best way for memorization. Memory works by association, so students must actively work to create some clever association between two or more concepts so that they can be remembered. The idea is to be creative and clever: just think of a picture that links pieces of information together, preferably something unusual or silly so it is more memorable (Tepperwein 2004).

Fox came up with the teaching style dimensions. He supposed that there is not one best way to teach, and he came with a concept of four different personal theories. For anatomy, his *transfer theory* (1983: 152) is applicable. According to this theory, teaching is about exposing information to students whereby the critical element is finding the best way to structure the information. The innovation of using mnemonics and 'making something' is a very good way to show the students how they can encourage imagination and improve remembering through associations.

The innovative intervention involved using some appropriate methods of associative learning that can enforce the process of remembering. It was inspired by Davies (2011: 1). Two methods were chosen from the multiple building ideas mentioned in her work: to use mnemonics and to increase imagination. Mnemosyne was the Greek goddess of memory, and her namesake, mnemonics, simply means 'memory aid'. Mnemonics are patterns or any clever learning technique that aids information retention. Most often, this pattern consists of letters or words. For example, the phrase "She Likes To Play Try To Catch Her" can be used to help students remember the order of the wrist bones: Scaphoid, Lunate, Triquetrum, Pisiform, Trapezium, Trapezoid, Capitate, Hamate bones. Mnemonics aim to translate information into an easier form to remember; thus the human brain can better retain and aid the transfer of information to long-term memory.

Imagination was increased during practical classes using the activity called 'make something.' This strategy required students to draw simple pictures or schemas of organs and their relationships with colored chalks on the blackboard; draw bones of the hand by using highlighters through dressed surgical gloves, or draw bones of the skull through dressed swimming cap; or to model the structures or organs of human body with plasticine. All these methods helped students to remember the difficult terms and to make anatomy more fun at the same time, despite the seriousness of this subject. These methods facilitated anatomy learning and the retention of important knowledge in the memory for as long as possible.

7.3 Research Design

Two methods were used to facilitate learning in this course: mnemonics and stimulation of imagination using 'make something' activity. The effect of the innovation on students' learning was measured by comparing the results of students who underwent the innovative method (I-group) with the results of students who did not receive the innovate intervention (N-group).

In this course students were assigned two theoretical written and two practical compulsory control tests. Each test covered the anatomical regions in a detailed and coherent manner. The theoretical test (which was given in the lecture) was composed of 100 statements; students had to assign them value true or false. The practical test (which was given during the practical class) consisted of 30 structures in a dissected body which students had to recognize and name.

The results after completing the written assessment test were compared. Each correct answer received 1 point, whereas incorrect and unmarked answers received 0 points. Students could pass the test with a minimum of 75 points.

Also, occasional short assessment tasks were given to students unexpectedly in both groups during the class to check the effectiveness of the innovative design. These tasks covered various content studied during the semester, but they were always the same for both groups. The overall results from I-group and N-group were compared. The results from the short tasks were not included in formal student assessment; they were used only to provide feedback on innovation for the teacher.

At the end of the semester, a short questionnaire was given to students in the I-group. Students had to answer three simple questions: Does it work better? Do you understand material more deeply and remember it for longer? Did you do better on your tests? The number of positive answers was compared with negative ones to verify observed changes in my teaching and in students' learning.

7.4 Findings

Two groups of students (N=38) were compared: 18 students from the I-group and 20 from the N-group took part in the same written test focusing on the thorax and its structures. In the I-group, 15 students passed the first test successfully and 3 students failed. Therefore, the success rate was 83%. In the N-group 16 students passed the test successfully, and 4 students failed, which implies a success rate of 80%. The overall majority of anatomy students from both groups who passed the test successfully reflected a similar result (81% in average). No significant difference existed between the results of I-group (who learned the basic structures of the human body through the innovative intervention) and N-group (who learned the structures through traditional methods).

In addition, seven unexpected short tasks were assigned during the semester. As it was mentioned before, they were the same for both groups of students. The total results between I-group and N-group were compared from each of them. For students to successfully pass the short assignment, they must have answered more than three quarters of the questions correctly. The results from both groups were very similar, with a mean score of 87% for the traditional group and a mean score of 88.3% for the innovative group. There were no significant differences in students' results, implying that students were able to learn anatomy independently of the method.

Contrary to this, students in the I-group perceived innovation very positively. 87% of students felt the new method had worked better, 98% thought they understood material more deeply and remembered it for longer and 93% said that had done better in the tests. From these results, it can be concluded that the activity of students increased during practical classes, and moreover, the students enjoyed the classes. This was a strong positive result of my innovation. Furthermore, the students taught by innovative methods based on using mnemonics and stimulated imagination said that they had enjoyed their in-class activity and spent less time with learning anatomy structures.

7.5 Limitation of the Study and Suggestions for Future Improvement

The major problem of higher education is an absence of teaching generic learning skills or 'teaching how to learn'. Learning is an inevitable and natural human activity; it is the central function of education. It is important to teach in a way that maximizes learning. All learning is self-directed in the sense that no-one can learn on behalf of another. Traditionally, higher education has emphasized individual learning and individualized assessment. The ideal learner is one who has the flexibility to select and adapt from a range of approaches, especially when encountering a novel situation or problem. According to Knapper (2004: 1), learning is most effective when there are intrinsic rewards for the learner, for example in terms of skill mastery, self-development, or self-esteem.

Regarding suggestions for future improvement, the research methods used to evaluate the results of the innovative intervention should be changed. The effect of the innovation was measured by comparing the results of the written test between two groups of students, students with innovative method and students without innovations in their classes. However, the difference in test results was not significant, so it is suggested that future research should also compare the time spent by each group in preparing for the test as well as the final test results between the experimental and control group. During this study, informal observation suggested that students learning in a traditional way had had more difficulties when learning anatomy, and so they spent more time to learn the structures and relationships among them. Formally assessing this is one way to possibly evaluate the effects of the innovation in the future.

7.6 Conclusion

The course which underwent this innovation was General and Oral Anatomy, a compulsory course for Dental Medicine students. The main problem of Anatomy education is how to secure long-term retention of essential knowledge. The innovative methods used in this study support the enhancement of memory by using mnemonics and by stimulating imagination during the teaching and learning process.

Mnemonics together with deep learning is a way to successfully study anatomy. This innovation showed success in increasing the interest of students as well as improving the quality of the class content. The new methods enabled students to feel interested in and to easily understand the topographical and functional relationships of anatomic structures without unnecessary memorization, and with an increase in the self-reliance of students on practical classes. The innovative methods helped students to learn human body structures in a more interesting way.

However, this method may be useful not only for anatomy teachers and students, but also for the teachers of other subjects, for example, the teachers of foreign languages. Playing with words is a funny and a spirited way to retain terminology in memory for a long time. After teaching by playing with words, learning has occurred more simply. It can be amusing to improve memory by using imagination. Activity and creativity together with experience enforce the learning process. Students liked all those experiences which helped them to learn and memorize. They enjoyed studying with passion and without stress, and they were ultimately looking forward to their anatomy class sessions.

References

Atherton, J. S. (2011): Learning and Teaching Bloom's Taxonomy. 7 January 2013, www.learningandteaching.info/learning/bloomtax.htm.

Biggs, J. (1999): Teaching for Quality Learning at University. Buckingham, UK: SRHE and Open University Press.

Davies, V. (2011): 'Teaching and learning in higher education. How do people learn?' Handout from the Summer school Teaching and Learning in Higher Education, Piešťany.

Fox, D. (1983): "Personal theories of teaching." Studies in Higher Education 8, 2, pp. 151-163.

Tepperwein, K. (2004):. Die Kunst mühelosen Lerners: Neue Lernmethoden machen es Ihnen leicht. München: Goldmann.

Majerník, J./Kluchová, D./Kozlíková, K. (2011) "3D Animations in education of medical students." Mefanet 2011 conference proceedings, MSD Brno, pp. 1-6.

8. Enhancing Students' Active Learning by Games

Martina Lučkaničová, Technical University of Košice

8.1 Introduction

The aim of this paper is to illustrate how students' active learning during seminars can be enhanced. It is based on experiences with teaching a rather theoretical course to two different groups of students (called groups A and B). As the course was rich in terminology, it was considered desirable to apply different activities to the seminars to make it more attractive for students. While doing so, it was perceived that different groups might react differently and therefore individual customization and flexible adaptation to the situation was considered necessary. Students' perceptions of the applied innovation were collected through continual feedback, and the final evaluation of the innovation was measured by questionnaires and the students' self-assessment at the end of the course.

The course Financial Investments is a compulsory course for Bachelor students of Finance, Banking and Investment. The target group of this course is a group of students in their third year of study (aged 18-22 years) who have little or no existing knowledge about investment. Students are supposed to build on their knowledge of statistics and apply it to managerial decision-making processes about investments. Before this, they are expected to acquire and comprehend the basic terminology within investment, become familiarized with the law about securities and investments in Slovakia and learn diverse methods of analysis used for market and financial instrument valuation. To understand financial investments is an essential prerequisite for the following Master's program, which goes more into depth on selected topics within investments and therefore builds on the previously acquired knowledge.

This course is taught in the form of lectures and seminars. It is organized under the control of the course coordinator, whose responsibility is to prepare the lectures and final examination, while the assistant professors and Ph.D. Students are responsible for the structure of the seminars. The distribution of the materials, such as written versions of lectures, presentations and other information is made through the Learning Management System, Moodle, which is used for courses across the faculty. The assessment design usually consists of 20 points for the written test and 80 points for the final oral exam.

Theoretical courses are usually less attractive to students, and few students show interest and passion for the topics in these types of courses. Students in such cases often demonstrate an indifferent attitude and learn just to achieve the minimum passing score. Not only the lectures, but also the seminars, are too theoretical, always taking the same monotonous format (explanation of the topic, repetition, assessment). The teacher, being at the centre of attention, plays the main and active role, which unfortunately, prevents students from active learning.

Having the chance to lead the seminars for the second time, it has been observed that the existing distribution of points was not motivating enough for students to learn on a regular basis. It is a frequent phenomenon at universities in Slovakia that students tend to take studying seriously only just before the exams. This causes stress and anxiety and has its impact on the knowledge and long-term retention.

When designing the teaching innovation, it was assumed that a change in the course structure and assessment would stimulate the students' curiosity for the subject, and motivate them to learn in a more active way and on a continual basis.

8.2 Aims of the Innovation and Theoretical Background

All the applied innovations were aimed at enhancing the active learning of students during seminars. Bonwell and Eison (1991) claim that active learning can encompass any instructional method that engages students in the learning process through meaningful learning activities and thinking about (reflecting on) what they are doing. Moreover, according to Stern and Huber (1997: 26) such learning has a significant impact on building rich and complex memory representations by enhancing all representations of individual long-term memory. These consist of semantic (definitions, concepts, principles), episodic (experiences linked to the concepts) and action representations (applied knowledge to solve problems) (Boekaerts and Simons 1993: 25).

The principal aim of redesigning the seminars was to help students to learn new knowledge through the enhancement of active learning. To achieve this, certain pedagogical goals were established, such as the enhancement of the intrinsic motivation of students to learn, the stimulation of students' activity and interest, and the development of cognitive competencies.

According to Knapper (2004: 1) learning becomes effective with *intrinsic motivation*, which can be initiated by regular feedback from the teacher and his or her demonstration of enthusiasm and commitment. Kvasz (2005: 22) defines intrinsic (internal) motivation as the one that is internal to the topic itself and therefore provokes students' interest and enthusiasm for learning.

The aim to stimulate students' intrinsic motivation was therefore addressed by incorporating various motivational inputs to the teaching and learning process. For example, within the first seminar, this was achieved by giving students the space to express their expectations and objectives with the purpose of finding the compromise for these at the beginning of the course. Similarly, the content of the session was presented at the beginning of each seminar so the students would know what to expect.

Regarding the structure of seminars, references to prior topics were made, and emphasis was placed on building knowledge linked to and based on this previously gained knowledge. To make the classes more interesting, different games were applied with diverse intentions: to link the theory with practice or simply to verify the comprehension of the theory.

Likewise, the assessment was adjusted in order to stimulate students' motivation. The original number of 20 points of the final grade to be earned in the seminars was raised to 30, and at the same time, it was divided into two parts: 15 points for in-class participation on seminars and 15 for testing the knowledge gained from the seminars at the end of semester. In this way, the active participation of students was rewarded in a way it had not been before. Besides increased motivation, it was expected that such distribution of points would lead to a more active attitude on students' part.

The redesigning of the structure of seminars was done according to *Bloom's taxonomy*. Bloom's taxonomy is considered to be a foundational classification of six cognitive levels of complexity that are involved in the process of learning. It is a hierarchical multi-tiered model that consists of knowledge, comprehension, application, analysis, synthesis and evaluation. According to the logic behind Bloom's taxonomy, one can master certain level only after passing through the levels before it. This model is widely used in course and curriculum designs because it presupposes the distribution of educational objectives into cognitive, affective and psychomotor domains, supporting a holistic form of education (Forehand 2005: 2).

In our case, attention was paid to competences such as knowledge, comprehension, application and, to a certain extent, analysis, excluding synthesis and evaluation as more advanced levels of learning that are more preferable for courses in which the goal is depth, rather than breadth of coverage of the material.

When designing seminars, the development of competencies was done according to Bloom's taxonomy, with regard to activities used in the seminars and the relevance of usage of Fink's three components of active learning (2003), namely: information and ideas, experience and reflective dialogue, in a variety of ways, including direct indirect and online.

Firstly, students were encouraged to advance their knowledge of the subject using various means. The theory presented by teacher on seminars was a direct form, the recommended textbooks and literature were an indirect form and material through the online learning platform Moodle and other recommended websites represented an online form of learning. Students could practice the comprehension of the theory by various games and activities during the seminars.

The name game is one example of such an activity. A note was stuck on each student's forehead with some term or concept from investments so that the holder of the note could not see it. The aim of the game was to make students guess what was written on their note card based on the explanation of the term provided by their schoolmates. Those terms that were not guessed correctly served as a good remark for teacher that they had not been understood properly and need revision.

Another example of a game that served to increase the activity of students during the seminar while acquiring new knowledge was a kind of competition, in which the proper formulation of questions by the teacher was crucial. It was already noted by Carin and Sund (1971: 39) that the quality of questions has a direct impact on the creation of an effective learning environment: "The questions a teacher asks can make the difference between an antiquated wasteland and an exciting learning environment." Hence the questions were carefully prepared in a way that students could find them both possible to answer and at the same time a little bit challenging.

Secondly, the comprehension and application of knowledge were supported by case studies, games and the final project, as an indirect form of learning by experience. One example of this type of game is the fill-in-the-blanks game. Students received cards with information about the current situation of some unspecified financial market instrument. They had to identify what specific type of instruments the articles were about. Articles were selected to enhance the breadth of views on investments and to give feedback to teacher about the general knowledge of students.

Moreover, in order to make students interested in the current worldwide investment situation, each seminar started with some short notice about a specific issue that was expected to be interesting for students. This interest-awaking activity was usually followed by a short discussion.

An out-of-class activity that aimed to support the same competencies (comprehension and application) was the project homework. First, students had to choose the financial market they would like to analyse, for example gold, silver, shares of specific company, forex, zinc, a commodity such as coffee, wheat, etc. Then, they were supposed to analyse the development of the price within the markets during the last year by using the data they could find on the internet as well as by applying knowledge they had already acquired during the seminars and lectures of this course. Students had three weeks to prepare their project, and they worked in pairs to complete this assignment.

Feedback on their project was offered with the time and possibility to make small adjustments before the final presentation. According to Knapper (2004: 2), constructive feedback and active listening are elements that can help students to improve their learning processes. Therefore, feedback was offered to students right after their presentations, considering both the content part (to highlight analytical skills) and the formal part (to highlight the presentation skills).

Thirdly, in order to develop the competencies of knowledge application and analysis, the dialogues and feedback on presentations from other students were expected to help, together with the self-reflection occurring during the self-assessment of each student's skills and abilities at the beginning and end of course.

To promote these competences, students were divided into smaller groups of four to participate in another type of activity. It was based on dividing the material to be learned into few logical parts, which were distributed to each group of students. The groups were supposed to learn their parts and then prepare a creative presentation in order to explain the material, such as investment process phases, types of financial markets, financial risks, financial market efficiency, shares and technical analysis, etc. For their colleague students. The criteria for assessment were discussed before the activity. During the preparation phase, the teacher's role was to facilitate students' discussions in order to clarify their doubts about their materials. After the presentations, the main parts of the given sub-topics were summarized by teacher, to make clear what was important.

In connection to this, Cohen (2008: 609), adopting the idea of Earl (2003), identifies three different types of assessment: the assessment of learning, assessment for learning and assessment as learning. The first one is the most frequently used and it is usually made in form of tests. Such assessment usually concentrates only on what was learned and does not help to identify the weaknesses of how the course was taught. The second one, assessment for learning, moves from a summative to a formative nature, enhanced by constant feedback that teacher provides to his or her students, so that assessment occurs on an on-going basis. The third form, assessment as learning, is considered to be the most rarely used. However, it is a very effective form of assessment, which, according to Cohen (2008: 610), occurs "when students personally monitor what they are learning and use the feedback from this monitoring to make adjustments, adaptations, and even major changes in what they understand." In regard to above mentioned activity, the second and the third types of Cohen's assessment were attempted to be applied.

After the presentations, constructive feedback was provided, stressing mainly the positive parts, while the negatives, which were common to all of the groups, were gently indicted at the end of all presentations. This type of feedback coincides with second type of assessment, called assessment for learning. At the end of the class, students were asked to evaluate themselves. The intention was to see whether they were able to do this critically by using so-called assessment as learning. It was expected that after the discussion about self-assessment, students would be able to formulate what the weak points of their presentations were and offer suggestions for improvement of their future work.

8.3 Research Design

The instruments that were used for evaluation of the innovation consisted of three types: the teacher's observation of student learning at seminars, a short informatory questionnaire that students were asked to fill out at the beginning and end of course and the final questionnaire at the end of the course.

The short, informatory, non-assessed questionnaire consisted of four items and had a self-evaluation nature. The items consisted of an open-ended question, two scale-type tasks and one creative task. The open-ended question was asked to monitor the current knowledge/comprehension of the topic, to check its level and homogeneity or heterogeneity of the group. Students were asked to describe what they thought financial investments were. In the second question the students were asked to evaluate the level of their knowledge about financial investments on a scale from 1 to 10. The third question, which asked students to self-evaluate their analytical skills using the same scale, was posed to define the "starting point" of students' analytical skills from their perspective. Within the last task students were asked to symbolically draw financial investment as they imagined it. The purpose of this task was to create a relaxed and accepting atmosphere while serving as an icebreaker activity, too.

The final questionnaire, consisting of 28 statements, was distributed to students during the last seminar. Students could express their agreement or disagreement with each of the statements on a five-point scale where 1 stood for "strongly disagree" and 5 for "strongly agree". The statements in the questionnaire covered the following topics: the course design, the achieved abilities/skills, the qualities of the teacher, the feedback provided and the overall satisfaction with the course.

8.4 Findings

The observation of students' activity and their learning at seminars brought several findings. During seminars, students' active involvement, increased enthusiasm, the enhancement of teamwork skills, and, finally, the developed ability to accept constructive feedback were observed.

Discussions about the current worldwide investment situation helped to outline the students' level of general knowledge. Besides this, the increased interest of students in the area of study could be observed. Those students active in discussions, showing the ability to go deeper into the topic, were sometimes provided with an extra task of explaining the topic to other students. As a result, these students felt honoured and their interest and enthusiasm were even more stimulated.

The increased ability of the students to work in teams was the side effect of the games and competitions. Students were motivated to work in small groups, discuss and listen to each other before they agreed on the final answer. Moreover, they had to respect their leader, as only the leaders were allowed to present answers to the teacher on behalf of their groups. It was perceived that students had really enjoyed these activities; they were vivid and open to discussing things they had not understood before.

The game in which the students were asked to prepare and explain the topic in the form of a presentation resulted in various outcomes. Some presentations were very entertaining but weak in terms of transmitting information. Other presentations were too dense with information, which could indicate that students did not think about what was really important and were not selective enough. There were also cases in which students simply read the theoretical parts aloud, rather than making an effort to remember their parts. However, students were led to self-assess their presentation, which in the end resulted in a double effect: they were able to accept constructive feedback from the teacher as well as to be critical about their own performance.

In summary, students, apart from acquiring basic knowledge concerning investments, managed to formulate their own views on the current financial situation. Many things that were going on, e.g. Financial crisis, different countries' strategies to deal with it, bond issues or countries' rating, served as good inputs for students' discussions. They were encouraged to express and argue for their opinions. They were gradually more and more open to taking an active role. Whereas at the beginning of the course, students tended to simply re-express what they read in the newspaper, by the end of the course, they had shifted to formulating more critical views on these issues.

In order to measure the subjectively perceived progress of students, a short informatory questionnaire was introduced at the beginning and at the end of the course. Even though both groups were taught in the same way in terms of methods and structure, the subjectively perceived progress by students in a group A differed from the perceptions of students in group B.

According to results concerning students' knowledge of financial investments, group A, had improved from an average of 3.6 to 7.3 on the scale 1 to 10 (where 10 refers to the most advanced). There was one student who expressed no difference in terms of gained knowledge before and after taking the course and five students expressed the biggest achieved difference of 5 points.

Group B considered itself to improve from 3.4 to 6.2 points. There were two students who perceived no difference between the level of their knowledge before and after taking the course, and the biggest achieved difference of 5 points on the scale was perceived by one student. Moreover, there was one student who showed a difference in the opposite direction, hence considering himself to have lost some knowledge, choosing a lower mark at the end than at the beginning. There were no doubts that different types of personalities and the team spirit, which was clearly reflected in the two different groups, affected teamwork, the learning atmosphere and therefore, to some extent, also influenced the perception of the learning progress.

Regarding the task to symbolically draw the financial investments, most of the students drew airplanes and themselves lying on the beach, expressing the sort of affluence acquired by investments. Comments of this type served as a good reference for the teacher during other seminars, when it was used as a motivating argument for investing effort in the comprehension of the topics.

The other tool used for the measurement of the innovation was the final questionnaire. It was distributed after the final test during the last class. The response rate of the group A was 91% (21 students) and the response rate of the group B was 82% (19 students). The results of the final questionnaire showed that, on average, the students were very satisfied with the teaching and learning methods, and that they felt an overall satisfaction with the course. For the purpose of this paper, only few items this questionnaire will be discussed.

The statement *"My professor tried to make this course and the subject material interesting"* received the highest score from both groups: group A with a value of 4.5 and group B with a value of 4.4. Selected statements and their average evaluation according to both groups are presented in Figure 7.

Both groups evaluated different elements of the course with similar marks, with only small deviations of 0.1 to 0.3 points. The most divergent perception (of 0.3 points) was in the case of *"developing teamwork skills," "the ability of the professor to answer all questions"* and *"the feedback provided on assignments"*. However, these results can be still considered to be positive as they received quite high average marks. The following statements received the lowest evaluation from both groups: *"This course has developed my ability to manage my time better"* (group A: 3.2, group B: 3.0), *"This course has helped me develop my ability to work on my own"* (group A: 3.3, group B: 3.2) and *"Where it was used, information technology helped me to learn"* (group A: 3.4, group B: 3.5).

Figure 7: The average evaluation distribution of selected statements from the course Financial Investments in winter semester 2011/2012.

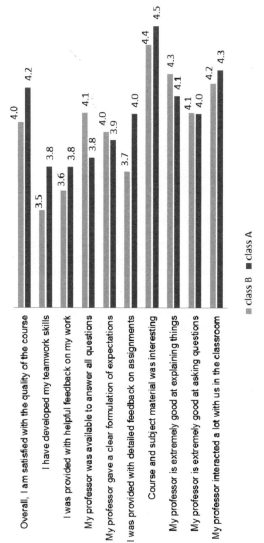

Source: own depiction

8.5 Limitations of the Study and Suggestions for Future Improvement

Despite the presented findings, the study revealed limitations of various types. First of all, it would be useful to run a longitudinal research study to evaluate the applied innovation that would systematically collect and verify teacher's perceptions on student learning. It is assumed that this would create the space for analysis of the implications of such innovations grounded in a more systematic and focused approach.

Secondly, comparing the on-going and final results of students in groups where the innovations were applied with the results of students in groups without the innovating elements could additionally lead to a more relevant way of measuring the impact of the innovation.

Furthermore, the redesign of the final questionnaire to focus more on the self- evaluation of students' progress would be more appropriate as well. All mentioned improvements would broaden the perspective about the innovations' effects, putting the emphasis on students' knowledge, skills and overall progress.

Lastly, considering the limitations of the innovation itself, it is necessary to mention financial resources. This fact was, for example reflected in the statement with one of the lowest scores from the final questionnaire, regarding the usage of the information technology in the teaching and learning process. Creating a learning environment involving modern information communication technologies apart from Moodle could serve as a highly motivational input for students. The higher budget would also create more possibilities to invite practitioners from the financial/investment sector who could offer students the opportunity to discuss the issues from a practical perspective. Having the chance to confront theory with practice could have an impact on the motivation to learn and could increase the attractiveness of the course.

During the implementation of the teaching innovation, two major problems arose; one was related to the character and the attitude of the groups, while the other to the internal organization of course.

Students appreciated that the seminars were carefully prepared, and above all, they liked the didactic games. However, the groups sometimes reacted in slightly different ways. In group A, the majority of students were relaxed; they always wanted to learn in a non-stressful and more playful way, and so the learning activities went smoother there. This group usually finished class on time and the learning atmosphere was generally positive. However, group B was sometimes more resistant, showing less interest in learning. It was clear that in this group, there was a lack of opinion leaders with a positive approach towards learning.

To solve the problem, it was at first necessary to understand the reasons that made the students behave in such a way. After feedback from students, it was detected that the problem was caused by the inconvenient time schedule of the seminars (late afternoon) and the fear of failure felt by some students due to the misunderstood assessment design under the terms of the point distribution. Once these problems were defined and addressed by the change of structure of seminars, putting the most challenging activities toward the beginning of the seminars and the re-explanation of the assessment design, the increased enthusiasm of students in this group could be observed.

The other adjustment which could contribute to the quality of the course was its internal organization. One of challenges for improvement would be, therefore, to strengthen the mutual cooperation and communication among all teachers teaching this course.

To conclude, some general suggestions for practice that emerged from experience with the implementation of this innovation could be summed up. First of all, it is advisable to be aware of the time schedule of courses when designing activities for the students because it can have direct impact on their willingness to cooperate and to take an active part. Similarly, the support of students' active participation at seminars and their motivation could be carried out by creating some activities in a form of competitions or games. Nevertheless, feedback also plays a very important role in terms of teaching and learning. For instance, frequently asking students for feedback can support the comprehension of their reactions, and, together with the teacher's observation, it can help to work on constant improvement.

On the other hand, students can be asked to self-assess their work, for example presentations, which may enhance their awareness of the strong and weak points and so to support the learning of formulating and accepting such feedback. Similarly, constructive feedback from teacher can significantly contribute to their improvement. Finally, the explaining and repeating of the assessment design may also avoid misunderstandings as students sometimes become very concerned with assessment, which negatively affects their work.

8.6 Conclusion

This chapter presents the experiences that have emerged from innovating the course of Financial Investments, an introductory but compulsory course for Bachelor students of Finance, Banking and Investment.

The main aim of the innovation was to enhance active learning of students during the seminars by focusing on their knowledge, comprehension and application, and by doing so, to improve their knowledge retention. A wide variety of activities was implemented in order to enhance students' motivation during seminars, such as the name game, the fill-in-the-blanks game, various types of competitions and the presentation of projects.

Based on the results, it could be concluded that the usage of a different structure of seminar, by applying various activities and learning methods, led to the enhancement of a positive learning atmosphere. Students' motivation and more active approaches also resulted from a better link between theory and practice as could be seen from discussions and analyses of the current worldwide situation. Moreover, the continual and mutual feedback between the teacher and students proved to be an important tool for enhancing the quality of learning.

References

Boekaerts, M./Simons, P. R. J. (1993): Leren en instructie: Psychologic van deleerling en het leerproces. Assen: Dekker & van der Vegt.

Bonwell, C. C./Eison, J. A. (1991): Active Learning: Creating Excitement in the Classroom. Higher Education Report No.1. George Washington University, Washington, DC: ASHEERIC Higher Education Report.

Carin, A. A./Sund, R. B. (1971): Developing questioning techniques: A self-concept approach. Columbus: C.E. Merrill Pub. Co. Quoted in Exley, K./Dennick, R. (2004) Small Group Teaching Tutorials Seminars and Beyond. London: Routledge.

Cohen, M. (2008) "Participation as assessment: Political science and classroom assessment techniques." Political Science 41, 3, pp. 609-612.

Earl, L. M. (2003): Assessment as Learning: Using Classroom Assessment to Maximize Student Learning. Thousand Oaks, CA: Corwin Press.

Fink, L. D. (2003): "A self-directed guide to designing courses for significant learning." In: Proceedings of the Workshop on Designing Courses (2003). San Francisco: Jossey-Bass, 2003. 15 February 2012, trc.virginia.edu/Workshops/2004/Fink_Designing_Courses_2004.pdf.

Forehand, M. (2005): "Bloom's taxonomy: Original and revised.' Quoted" In: Orey, M. (ed.): Emerging perspectives on learning, teaching, and technology. 31 October 2012, projects.coe.uga.edu/epltt/.

Knapper, CH. (2004): "Research on College Teaching and Learning: Applying What We Know." Discussion paper for the Teaching Professor Conference. Philadelphia, May 21-24, 2004. 12 March 2012, cll.mcmaster.ca/scholarship/pdf/research_on_college_teaching.pdf.

Kvasz, L. (2005): "On possible approaches to motivation." In: Gregušová, G. (ed.): How to Teach Political Science? Experience of The Experience of First-time University Teachers. Epsnet Teaching Political Science series no.1, Budapest: epsnet, pp. 21-26.

Stern, D./Huber, G., L. (1997): "Active learning for students and teachers." In: Reports from Eight Countries, OECD. Frankfurt and New York: Peter Lang, 1997. 4 March 2012, deanproject.eu/turkish/pdfs/23004.pdf.

Section 4: Enhancing Student Abilities of Theory Application

9. Worksheets as a Method of Helping Students to Apply Theory

Anna Vallušová, Matej Bel University in Banská Bystrica

9.1 Introduction

This paper describes an innovative approach to leading the seminars of Microeconomics I. It stresses the necessity to involve students consciously in the learning process and to interconnect economic theory and real world processes. The paper also presents the experiences from the application of this approach into practice. To confirm the hypothesis that activating methods can lead to better ability to apply the gained knowledge to specific problem-solving tasks, a comparison of average grades (before and after the innovation) was used. The paper, finally, proposes possibilities for further application of this approach and its improvement.

Microeconomics I. Is a mandatory course for students in their first year of study. The course focuses on the basic terminology, principles, and ways of thinking which economists use. Therefore, it is obligatory for all students within each study program, including Business, Tourism and Public Economics.

The course is divided into two lectures and two seminars per week. The lecture is held for approximately two hundred students at once. The aim of the lecture is to introduce basic ideas in given area of economic science. It is held by a senior lecturer or a professor. For the seminars, the students are divided into groups of approximately 30 students. Three or four assistant professors and Ph.D. Students are usually responsible for leading the seminars. The seminars are focused on the application of the theory by completing problem-solving tasks. The course is assessed by two written tests, which consist of problems similar to those practiced during the seminars. This method has been used for a long time without any updating; therefore, it does not address current problems in the economy or modern trends in teaching the basics of Economics.

For these reasons, it was necessary to addresses three challenges. The first challenge was grounded in students' passive learning. Students tended to focus on the skill of "how to solve exercises," rather than learning "how to think like an economist." This seemed to be caused by the type of assessment used, which was not motivating enough for adopting the latter approach.

Secondly, the fact that academic courses of Microeconomics usually presuppose some previous knowledge of this subject was rather problematic. This presupposition is often false because the majority of the students had previously studied at a grammar school in which Economics was just a minor part of one subject. The content of this subject is typically informative, rather than offering a solid basis in the disciplinary principles and assumptions required for an intermediate academic course. The absence of this basis was problematic because in Economics, as in any social science, it is impossible to achieve a universal truth and therefore a focus on assumptions is crucial.

The final challenge was that students could not make connections between theory and real world processes. This problem was caused by the fact that economists often describe reality using economic models, and the students rarely make the connection between these models and phenomena they know from practice, for example, their behaviour as a customer. The main reason for this situation is the fact that Economics uses terminology and methodology which differ from those commonly used in grammar schools.

9.2 Aims of the Innovation and Theoretical Background

In this context, it was possible to define two goals of the innovation: one at the level of knowledge, and the other at the level of values and approaches. The first goal was to eliminate the students' passive learning; the second was a need to support students' understanding of what Economics was about and what the connections between the economic theory and real world processes were. These aimed to result in an increased in-class participation of the students and their improved performance on the final exam.

The idea behind these goals is the general belief that the proper understanding of the principles of Economics contributes to sustainable development of society. The necessity of questioning the foundations of the current streams in Economics was shown clearly by the recent economic and financial crisis, which is often referred to as a crisis of values. Vaiman and Sigurjonsson (2011) emphasize the importance of education in influencing the business environment, especially in small societies like the society in Slovakia. They claim that "it is the responsibility of business educators to show the students how mistakes have influenced both the business and the societal environments in the past, so that similar missteps are not repeated in the future" (Vaiman and Sigurjonsson 2011: 348).

Audebrand and Burton (2011: 358) stress the necessity of embedding the economic theory in a broader context because, as they state, "the use of mathematical models to the exclusion of other ways of framing their activities allowed countless participants in the financial markets to completely ignore the ethical implications of what they were doing". Similarly, Horeháj and Kubišová (2011: 48) pointed out that oversimplification leads to interpreting economic terms as "value neutral and it provokes an impression of explicitness".

The courses which focus on the principles of Economics, including for example Micro- and Macroeconomics, General Economic Theory, or Principles of Economics, are in general, different from other courses taught at schools with economic curricula. It is useful to be aware of this difference when teaching such a course. Economic curricula are usually oriented toward practical skills. Typical representatives of such curricula include courses like Business Economics, Accounting, Management, Marketing, etc. It does not mean that these courses do not contain any theory, but rather that they deal with specific types of firms, environmental settings, legal frameworks, etc.

On the other hand, foundational or principle courses, such as Microeconomics, deal with the philosophical foundations of the economic disciplines. As Yuenegert (2009: 2) states, "the principle courses offer a set of insights into the functioning and failures of market and governments, and the consequences of human interdependence in the economy, which together provide fruitful framework for understanding and analysing the social order and the role of business in that order."

These courses use more advanced terminology as well as economic models, which seem to be separated from reality. In fact, however, they try to express reality in a more exact way. It means that these courses have the potential to become a fascinating synthesis of psychology, sociology, philosophy and common sense which allow us to "understand the world in which we live" (Mankiw 1998: 519). Nevertheless, there is a danger (mainly because of terminology and methodology), that they remain misunderstood as a set of ideas separated from reality.

A crucial input for the innovative teaching and learning design was the assumption about the students whom the innovation was supposed to target. Hamermesh (2002: 449) proposed that it is useful for instructors to prepare lessons with three main assumptions in mind: that most of the students "(i) do not intend to take more Economics; (ii) know very little about what Economics is really about; and (iii) are very concerned about maintaining/ raising their grade point averages." That is why he suggested using engaging examples to demonstrate the connection with reality, "ideas at frontiers of economic research," which can demonstrate the power and "excitement" of economic analysis. He also advised to prepare the seminar in such a way that the main points can be summarized in three or four sentences.

Box 1: Worksheet fragment: Learning Objectives

I. Learning Outcomes – Introduction to economics

After studying this topic, you should be able to:

- ✓ Explain how economics is useful as a science;
- ✓ Define the scarcity problem and illustrate it using production possibility frontier;
- ✓ Describe methods of economic research and identify some pitfalls of economic analysis;
- ✓ Use the graphs as a basic tool for describing phenomena in the economy.

Frank (2005) introduced a similar approach to teaching economics. He pointed out the fact that students usually "find it easier to process information in narrative form than in more abstract form like equations and graphs" (Frank 2005: 1). That is why he preferred explaining economic processes using the form of a story and requested the same from the students in their assignments. He claimed that "learning Economics is like learning language: real progress in both cases comes only from speaking" (Frank 2005: 1).

Box 2: Worksheet fragment: Assigned reading

II. The assigned reading – History of economic theories

Tomáš Sedláček: The secret force of the stories

It would be foolish to assume that economic inquiry began with the scientific age. At first, myths and religions explained the world to people who asked basically similar questions as we do today; today science plays that role.

The study of the history of a certain field is not, as is commonly held, a useless display of its blind alleys or a collection of field′s trials and errors (until *we* got it right). History of thoughts helps us helps us to get rid of the intellectual brainwashing of the age, to see through the intellectual fashion of the day, and to take a couple of steps back.

Studying old stories is not only benefit for historians, or for understanding the way our ancestors thought. These stories have their own power, even after new stories appear and replace or contradict them. An example could be drawn from the most famous dispute in history: the dispute between the story of geocentrism and the story of heliocentrism. As everyone knows, in the battle between helio- and geocentrism, the heliocentric story won, though even today we geocentrically say that the Sun *rises* and *sets*. But the Sun does not rise or set: if anything is rising, it's our Earth (around the Sun), not the Sun (around the Earth).

(Sedláček 2011: 5, abridged)

These theoretical principles were applied by designing special worksheets. These worksheets were available for students in advance, a week before the seminar. Each of them consisted of three main parts. Firstly, there were three to five teaching objectives to be achieved in the form of crucial information to be remembered, understood and applied (example in Box 1). Their purpose was to shift the attention of the students from the procedures of problem solving to the understanding of a phenomenon, which the procedure could offer.

The next part of the worksheet was an assigned reading. It consisted usually of one or two short stories or blogs (1/2 – 1 page) written by a well-known economist, dealing with the topic of the seminar in an untraditional way (example in Box 2). The texts were written in light, non-academic style, so they were assumed to be quite easy to understand. The purpose of the reading was to introduce a given topic to the students in popular way and in language they could understand in order to arouse their interest.

The last part of the worksheet consisted of a problem set — exercises from practice which could be completed by using a given theory (example in Box 3). Great attention was paid to the formulation of the exercises to be as understandable and as imaginable as possible. The exercises were designed to describe situations which could be experienced by the students in their life in order to make a clear connection between theory and practice. Students were supposed to prepare the solution in advance to be able to discuss and concentrate on the problematic issues in their seminar. In order to motivate students to do so, they had an opportunity to gain five extra points per semester, depending on the level of their participation in the classes.

Box 3: Worksheet fragment – Assigned reading

III. The problem set – Costs, Revenues and Profit
1.   Consider running a business – a small café near your dormitory. Assume you can sell 200 cups of coffee a month; it means you can gain a revenue of 300 €. You need to pay 200€ for the material and the rent. You will serve your customers yourself, so you do not need to pay anybody, however you will spend 80 hours monthly in your café. If you get a part time job in a supermarket, you can earn 2€ per hour. What are your explicit and implicit costs and accounting and economic profit? Are you going to run such a business?

9.3 Research Design

In order to evaluate the effects of the innovation, two methods were used. Firstly, student behaviour, participation, and feedback in the seminar were observed, and the findings were compared with the experiences from the previous year, when students were taught in the traditional way.

The second way of evaluating the innovation was the comparison of average marks from final tests between the classes with and without the innovation (from the previous year). It was assumed that understanding of learning objectives would be a more effective way of studying for the test than learning-by-heart techniques students used in the past. (From the experience, the students tend to use memorizing until they are forced by an external factor for example, by their teacher or by failing the exam to switch to another approach, simply because it is easier for them and they are used to this approach from grammar school.)

The test consisted of two types of tasks: questions typically asking students to write definitions and assigned problems. This means that approximately 40% of the total points could be gained from questions focused on definitions, where memorizing is a better approach to learning, while 60% could be achieved from questions for which deep understanding is a better strategy. As the threshold for passing the test was 65%, it can be said that deep understanding is a key to passing the test; however, memorizing is the key to improving a grade.

9.4 Findings

Subjectively perceived, the innovation contributed to higher participation of the students during the seminars. The methods used (designing the worksheets, class participation points, focus on stories, etc.) Indirectly led to clearer rules during the lesson. The teacher knew what to expect from students, and the students knew what to expect from the teacher. This contributed to an agreeable and cooperative atmosphere at the seminars and the elimination of communication barriers between the teacher and the students.

These facts were especially observable within the group of students who had not passed the course in their first year of study and had to repeat it. All of them shared, negative attitudes toward the course at the beginning and found it both boring and unimportant for their future career. However, it was mainly these students who showed their surprise and enthusiasm when they had realized that certain theories corresponded with phenomena they knew from real life.

Focusing on the "student-friendly" formulation of exercises also turned out to be useful. As the problems were familiar to students, they did not hesitate to contribute to the discussions. They started to interconnect their own experiences with economic models.

To comment on the results of the final test, the average mark of the students who experienced the innovation (the average was made just from the marks of the student who passed the test) was slightly worse – it went down from 2.25 to 2.55 on a 3 point scale in comparison to previous year results. However, the number of students who did not pass the test decreased from eight students in the previous year to one student the year the innovation was introduced. This means that 95% of the students passed the test in comparison to the previous year, when only 58% of the students succeeded.

9.5 Limitations of the Study and Suggestions for Future Improvement

The experiences from implementing the innovation to seminars of Microeconomics show a broad area for improvement.

To start with, it is necessary to rethink the way of assessment including feedback to the students during the seminar to support their learning. The possibility to gain five points for the activity and participation during the whole semester was insufficient and not motivating enough for two reasons. Firstly, it is a very small part of final grade; secondly, it did not allow stimulation of the quality of participation, only the quantity. Moreover, it was based only on the subjective opinion of a teacher, which was considered confusing by students as they did not know the exact criteria.

On the other hand, the format of the seminar and teaching method turned out to be a more important motivating factor than the threat of losing five points from the final score. However, students' continuous preparation for the seminar and the feedback from the teacher could improve the effectiveness of the learning process even more. This could be achieved by redesigning the assessment and grading process by allocating more points (at least 40%) for work in the seminars. Naturally, in that case, assigning participation points could not be based on the teacher's subjective evaluation but rather on completing tasks which both check students' understanding and lead to mutual feedback among teacher and students. An example of such a task could be finding a newspaper article connected to the theory discussed that week and formulating a forecast of future consequences using the theory.

To continue, the potential of assigned readings was not wholly used during the seminars. Their role was to attract the attention of students toward economic issues and increase their interest in the area of research. However, as the readings were not further used during the seminar, the students found it useless to read them. It would be probably more effective to work with the texts during the seminar and to prepare the questions for discussion or problems based on the reading.

To conclude, the tools for evaluating the aims of the innovation should to be redesigned in order to show more accurately the results of the new teaching methods and the areas for further improvement. The first measurement of the innovation was based solely on subjective evaluation, while the second part, although using quantitative methods, failed to show explicit correlation between the innovation and the test results of the students. Moreover, the research reflected solely the achievement of the goals connected to student knowledge, not the goals connected to their values and approaches. Therefore, it is necessary to design a new set of indicators in the level of values and approaches and an effective way to measure it. The stress should be put mainly on the "development of critical thinking and ability to ask new questions and seek answers to them" (Marasová and Horehájová 2009: 3).

In general, the implementation of such innovations was especially demanding on the personality and performance of the teacher. The main reason is that the students frequently felt uncomfortable when the learning activity differed from the model they had been used to (sitting, listening, answering questions). They were pulled out from their comfort zone and involved in something which was not familiar to them. The aim of the activating method was to gain students' trust, to motivate them to take part in a learning style that they had never experienced before.

To achieve this, a little bit of humor and informality, ordinarily, helps much. However, there is a danger that the "humorous ice-breaking" may distract students' attention from the goal of the lecture. For this reason, it is useful to set clear, goal-oriented rules at the beginning of the course. They should regulate the way of preparing for the seminar, the expected form of participation and class performance, the ways of giving mutual feedback, as well as sanctions for breaking the rules. Paradoxically, clear rules often reduce tension in the teacher-student relationship because they all know what to expect.

9.6 Conclusion

Most economic curricula at universities contain a course dealing with the principles of economics. In this report an innovative approach to the course Microeconomics I. Using activating methods was described. It is a compulsory course for the first year students of the Faculty of Economics, during which they should acquire basic economic terminology and master the way of economic thinking. The approach was designed to address three teaching problems: (i) students' passive learning, (ii) a false presupposition of previous knowledge of the subject and (iii) students lacking ability to make connections between economic models and practice.

The innovation consisted in designing and using worksheets for students, which consisted of three parts: learning objectives, assigned reading and a problem set. To design them, the following activating principles were applied. Firstly, to increase students' interest in content, the ideas at the frontier of economic research were used within the assigned readings. Secondly, to enhance understanding of the topic and interconnection with practice, the seminars were designed in the way that it was possible to summarize their objectives in three to five sentences. Particular economic processes were explained in a narrative way and the formulation of exercises allowed students to use experiences from their life to solve them.

In general, the innovation can be considered to be successful. The most important achievement is the fact that it led to creating a learning atmosphere in the classroom in which the students had no barriers to ask questions and contribute to the discussion. The effectiveness of the innovation was confirmed by the comparison of test results with the previous year, which showed that considerably more students were able to pass the final exams as the result of proposed teaching methodology. However, it also revealed areas for improvement, mainly in the process of students' evaluation, which should lead to mutual feedback between teacher and students.

References

Audebrand, L. C./Burton, J. W. (2011): "Nurturing integrity in management education with the development of an alternative web of metaphors." In: Wankel, C./Stachowicz-Stanusch, A. (eds.): Handbook of Research on Teaching Ethics in Business and Management Education. Hershey: IGI Global, pp. 357-371.

Frank, R. (2005) "Students Discover Economics in Its Natural State." 16 October 2012, www.nytimes.com/2005/09/29/business/29scene.html.

Hamermesh, D. S. (2002) "Microeconomic principles teaching tricks." The American Economic Review 2, 92, pp. 449-453.

Horeháj, J./Kubišová, Ľ. (2011): "Individualistic mentality and economic education." E+M 4, 14, pp. 46-53.

Mankiw, N. G. (1998): "Teaching the principles of economics." Eastern Economic Journal 4, 24, pp. 519-524.

Marasová, J./Horehájová, M. (2009): Microeconomics. Banská Bystrica: EF UMB.

Sedlacek, T. (2011): Economics of Good and Evil. New York: Oxford University Press.

Vaiman, V./Sigurjonsson, T.O. (2011): "Rethinking ethics education in business schools in the post-financial crisis epoch." In: Wankel, C./Stachowicz-Stanusch, A. (eds.): Handbook of Research on Teaching Ethics in Business and Management Education. Hershey: IGI Global, pp. 342-356.

Yuengert, A. (2009): "Teaching the Introduction to Microeconomics Course in the Catholic Business Curriculum" 16 October 2012, www.stthomas.edu/cathstudies/CST/curriculum/portlandcurr/Yuengertbackgroundwresponse2.pdf.

Section 5: Making Assessment an Effective Tool for Student Learning

10. Bloom's Taxonomy as an Organizing Principle of an Assessment Innovation

Terézia Repáňová, Matej Bel University in Banská Bystrica

10.1 Introduction

The aim of this paper is to discuss a course innovation by changing the assessment criteria according to Bloom's taxonomy. Two main teaching challenges were addressed: one was related to the lack of student motivation and the second to the change of the traditional assessment criteria, which did not enhance students' motivation. Accordingly, two groups of innovative teaching methods were introduced. The success of the innovation was measured by a non-standardized final questionnaire and by the subjective observation of the teacher. The results showed that the students moved from the stage of *remembering* to the stage of *analysing* in Bloom's taxonomy. Presentations, quizzes and games seemed to be the most helpful innovation activities.

The course Urban and Cultural Tourism is an optional 5 ECTS credit course for the first year MA students. The course has been taught in English and it consists of lectures held every other week and of weekly seminars. The course aims to provide students with background knowledge about urban and cultural tourism and the supply and demand for this type of tourism. It introduces the students to the interpretation of cultural heritage as well as to the marketing of the city. An emphasis is placed on the students' analysis of cultural and urban tourism in the chosen city/town. The department was offering this type of the course for the second time. There were eight students in the class.

The usual practice of assessment in this course was grounded in the traditional assessment criteria, namely two tests during the semester (usually one in the middle and one at the end of semester) and one student presentation. Students, however, often seemed to be bored during presentations lasting too long (either the teacher's lecture, or other students' presentations). Having the experience of teaching the same course a year before, a number of teaching challenges were observed: the necessity to increase the students' motivation and to change the traditional assessment criteria.

10.2 Aims of the Innovation and Theoretical Background

Drawing on the identified teaching challenges, the aim was to avoid the kind of traditional assessment based on memorizing the facts in the middle and at the end of semester and at the same time to increase the attention of students during their colleagues' presentations. The process of the course preparation was initiated by redesigning the whole course first, starting with the identification of the aims and learning outcomes, followed by establishing the assessment criteria. These were designed to help students learn continuously throughout the semester instead of overloading them in the middle and at the end of semester and in this way to motivate them to become more attentive and have a more active approach.

The formulated aims and learning outcomes were aligned to the assessment criteria (Morgan et al. 2004: 214) and learning activities (Table 1).

Table 1: The connection between learning outcomes, assessment criteria and student activities.

Learning outcomes	Assessment criteria	Learning activities
Describe the specifications of the urban and cultural tourism.	Quizzes	"Fill-in-the-blanks", Games
Identify the supply and demand for urban and cultural tourism.	Quizzes, Presentation	"Fill-in-the-blanks", Games
Analyse the marketing tools in the chosen city/town.	Final draft of case study	"Fill-in-the-blanks", Games, Case study research and writing
Review the situation of urban and cultural tourism in the chosen city/town.	Final presentation + written paper	Peer assessment, Games
Design the vision for how to attract more visitors to the cities.	Final presentation + written paper	Peer assessment

Source: own depiction

In order to prevent students from pure memorization of facts, *Bloom's taxonomy* (Moore and Stanley 2009: 2) was used to redesign the assessment criteria. Bloom's taxonomy is a classification of learning objectives within education. Moreover, it provides a useful structure in which a course assessment can be categorized. At the bottom of the taxonomy is the stage *remembering* (at which the student can remember the information), followed by *understanding* (explaining ideas or concepts), *applying* (transferring the knowledge into practical situations), *analysing* (comparing or organizing things), *evaluating* (the student can provide judgments or critique) and finally the stage of the *creating* (at which the student can design new ideas or concepts).

As the course was designed for the first year MA students, who were already able to remember and understand the basic terminology, the attention moved from basic levels to more advanced levels. For this reason, the final grade was composed from the results from quizzes (which represented the lowest stages in Bloom's taxonomy – *remembering* and *understanding*), a presentation and case study (the stages applying and analysing), a final presentation of the project and a written paper (the stages *evaluating* and *creating*). In this way, each stage was aligned to a concrete assessment tool (Figure 8).

Figure 8: The connection between Bloom's taxonomy and assessment criteria

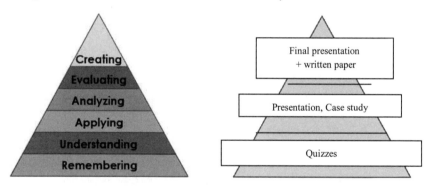

Source: own depiction after Overbaugh and Schultz 2012

According to Dewey (Exley and Dennick 2004: 35) the process of education must start with the interests of the learner, followed by thinking and activity. Because in the past noticeable interest of the students was not observed, two groups of innovation activities were created. The tools in the first group aimed to help students to think and become more engaged. These were the quizzes at the beginning of each seminar, presentations of the chosen topics, case studies and games.

Firstly, ten minute-long quizzes were held at the beginning of each seminar. Each quiz consisted of five open-ended questions, related to the topic from the last session and evaluated on a five-point scale. Secondly, students had to present a chosen topic. The presentation skills of the student and the content were evaluated by the teacher and partially by students. The third tool used to increase engagement was a short case study provided by the teacher. Students working in pairs were asked to present their results. This activity, among others, was expected to develop student ability to work in a team.

The second group of tools was planned to increase students' attention, because many of them usually became bored during long lectures or during their colleagues' presentations. To avoid this, two types of activities were created: fill-in-the-blanks activities during lectures and peer assessment of their colleagues' presentations. These activities were not part of the student grade.

The aim of the fill-in-the-blanks activity was to motivate students to attend the lecture, at which background knowledge was presented. Students were sent the frame of the lecture in advance in order to print it out and bring to the lecture. The frame consisted of the content of the lecture with some words and definitions intentionally left out.

The other attention-catching activity was peer assessment of their colleagues' presentations. During each student's presentation, the rest of the class evaluated his or her presentation skills and the content. A list of factors to be evaluated (eye contact, audibility, articulation, layout and the content) was given to students in advance. All eight students presented at one seminar. The student who had achieved the highest number of points was given an award.

10.3 Research Design

The success of the innovation was measured by two methods: the teacher's subjective observation and a questionnaire distributed to the students at the last seminar. The final questionnaire consisted of four items, and the 100% return of all the questionnaires was ensured by making its submission worth two points of students' final grade.

On the first item, the students were asked to evaluate several statements on a Likert-type scale from 1-5, where 1 meant "entirely false" and 5 meant "entirely true". The statements were designed according to Bloom's taxonomy, where the first statement matched the bottom of the hierarchy (see Figure 9). This question format was used for all the statements. The aim of this question was to find out if the students understood the intention of leading them to the highest possible levels of the hierarchy.

The second item of the questionnaire dealt with the question of to what extent the applied tools (teaching innovations) helped students to understand the subject better. The students were asked to evaluate whether the tasks helped them to better understand the material covered during the course. They evaluated the presentations, peer assessment activity, quizzes, fill-in-the-blanks activity and games at the seminars on the Likert-type scale from 1-5, where 1 meant "did not help me at all" and 5 meant "helped me the most".

Figure 9: The connection between the statements from the questionnaire and Bloom's taxonomy.

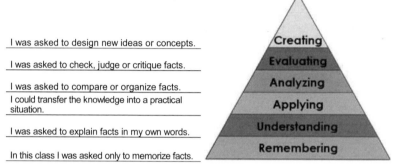

Source: own depiction after Overbaugh and Schultz 2012

The third question was an optional comment box, in which students could express their dis/satisfaction with the tools used. The last question of the questionnaire served as a space for students to write their suggestions for course improvement.

10.4 Findings

The observation proved that students had no problems working on the levels of remembering, understanding, applying and analysing. However, students found it difficult to work on the levels evaluating and creating, which was noticeable in tasks based on critical thinking and designing new concepts.

In order to process the results from the questionnaires, the points students assigned to each statement were summed and averaged. The maximum number of points for each statement (Table 2) and the evaluation of the innovative activities (Table 3) was five.

According to the results, students thought they were mostly asked to compare or organize facts (which correspond to the stage of *analysing* in Bloom's taxonomy). In second place was the opportunity to explain facts in their own words (which relates to the stage of *understanding*). Further, students appreciated the possibility to check, judge and critique facts together with transferring knowledge to practical situations. These two statements received a similar number of points and they correspond to the stages *evaluating* and *applying*. The task to design new ideas and concepts was in the second-to-last place, followed by the memorization of facts.

Table 2: The interpretation of the first question

Statement	Average points from students	Place
I was asked to design new ideas, new concepts.	2.50	4.
I was asked to check, judge or critique some facts.	3.25	3.
I was asked to compare or organize facts.	5.00	1.
I could transfer the knowledge into a practical situation.	3.25	3.
I was asked to explain facts in my own words.	4.75	2.
I was asked only to memorize facts.	2.25	5.

Source: own depiction

To comment on the results of the students' statement about memorizing facts (which received the minimum average score), the results proved that the effort to move students' learning to the higher levels of the taxonomy was successful. On the other hand, students assigned fewer points on average to the learning outcome of designing new ideas or concepts (being one of the teacher's goals). One explanation of such a result might be that the end of the course, aiming at the designing the students' visions, was led by another teacher, what unfortunately limits our possibility of its interpretation.

In order to process the students' evaluation of the innovative activities (Table 3), a similar approach was taken. Students were asked to assign five points at maximum to each innovative activity. The results were summed and averaged.

The quizzes, used mostly to motivate students to memorize the terminology and make them attentive during the class, were highly popular. The fact that they touched the level of remembering, which students have already mastered, could have highly contributed to such a result.

The presentations, which students were also used to, were, according to the results, helpful and welcomed. One of the problems, however, was their inappropriate duration, which often exceeded the time limit. The other problem was concerning the students' presentation skills. Although the topic was well prepared, usually the eye contact with the audience was missing.

Students appreciated games at the seminar (crosswords, connecting words or categorizing the terms into the groups), because they could help them to remember the facts more easily. Some of the games were shown on the slides, while others were printed in advance and distributed at the seminar. Both forms proved to be interesting for the students.

Table 3: The interpretation of the second question

Innovative activities	Average points from students	Place
Presentations	4.62	1.
Quizzes	4.12	2.
Games at the seminar	4.00	3.
Peer assessment activity	3.37	4.
Fill-in-the-blanks activity	2.75	5.

Source: own depiction

From the second group of innovations, the peer assessment activity seemed to be a little bit confusing. When asked to point to the positives and negatives of their colleagues' way of presenting, students usually found everything positive and did not say anything negative. The problem could have been in the way of setting the task. Instead of asking students to say something positive and negative about their colleagues' presentation, it would be probably more effective to ask, what they would improve on the presentation. Another solution could be to ask students for a short anonymous written feedback. To achieve the highest response rate, the teacher could note down each student's submission. Despite this, this innovation achieved its aim to make students pay attention during the presentations.

The fill-in-the-blanks activity at the lectures achieved the lowest number of preference points. This could have been caused by the fact that the chosen terms were left out on almost every slide of the presentation. The fill-in-the-blanks task, not always simple, had the aim of motivating students to think about the presented topic more attentively. Students, however, suggested that the missing words in the presentations were sometimes too difficult. Nevertheless, this could be also because this activity was new for students. A better way, as one of the students suggested, could be a crossword or game at the end of the lecture. On the other hand, the sessions were held in English which might have been a problem for non-native speakers as well. In order to overcome this difficulty, students can be asked to bring a dictionary to the seminar or a teacher could prepare a short list of terms for each session.

10.5 Limitations of the Study and Suggestions for Future Improvement

Some elements of the innovation proved to be effective, while others would need a slight modification.

The activities of the highest contribution to the stated aim were the presentations and the quizzes. Subjective observation and also the questionnaire demonstrated the achievement of their purpose. As suggested above, some activities, such as the fill-in-the-blanks task or the peer evaluation would be more efficient if reworked.

Another area that would also need an adjustment is the time management of missed obligations for the students who were sick or missed the seminar because of other reasons. For those who missed the quiz, a short essay might be appropriate. The essay could relate to the topic of the class and should be described in the syllabus, together with the expected extent. A suggestion for the future improvement of the lecture is a *feedback lecture* (Schurr 1999: 106). A feedback lecture is a method by which the students are asked to listen for just 25-30 minutes and then to note as much as they have remembered. After the lecture, students spend time in small groups, reconstructing the missing information. This method would help students to concentrate and work in a team.

The study was, however, limited by the fact that the end of the course had to be, due to personal reasons, taught by another teacher. This prevented the full realization of the teaching innovation and therefore, also, the achievement of the goals.

10.6 Conclusion

The innovated course Urban and Cultural Tourism was designed for the first year MA students. There were two main challenges perceived during teaching the course in the past. On the one hand, students seemed unmotivated at the lectures and the seminars. On the other hand was the traditional assessment criteria usually used in the teaching at the university, which failed to enhance students' motivation.

The tools that aimed to help the students to become active at the seminars and to pay attention at the lectures were designed according to Bloom's taxonomy. These were quizzes, presentations, case study presentations, fill-in-the-blanks activity and peer evaluation activity. At the same time it was necessary to help students to move from the stage of remembering to the higher levels of Bloom's taxonomy. This was achieved through the corresponding choice of the assessment criteria.

According to the results from the questionnaire, the students thought they had mostly been asked to compare or organize facts (which corresponds to the stage of analysing in Bloom's taxonomy). The task to design new ideas and concepts, corresponding to the stage of creating was in second-to-last place. Even though the aim to markedly reach the highest levels of Bloom's taxonomy was not fulfilled, the students made visible progress to more complex learning processes.

From the innovation tools, students marked as the most helpful activities in the following order: the presentations, quizzes, games at the seminar, peer assessment activity and fill-in-the-blanks activity. The tools used proved to be a useful way of increasing students' motivation and attention.

References

Exley, K./Dennick R. (eds) (2004): Small Group Teaching. London: Routledge.

Moore, B./Stanley, T. (2009): Critical Thinking and Formative Assessment: Increasing the Rigor in your Classroom. New York: Eye On Education.

Morgan, C./Dunn, L./Parry, S./O'Reilly, M. (2004): The Student Assessment Handbook. London: Routledge

Overbaugh, R.C./Schultz, L. (2012): "Bloom's taxonomy." Old Dominion University. 30 September 2012, ww2.odu.edu/educ/roverbau/Bloom/blooms_taxonomy.htm.

Schurr, S. L. (1999): "Interactive lectures." In: Totten, S./Johnson, C./Morrow L. R./Sills-Briegel, T (eds.): Practicing What We Preach: Preparing Middle Level Educators. London: Routledge, pp. 106-108.

11. Teaching Academic Writing Effectively

Miroslava Petáková, Catholic University of Ružomberok

11.1 Introduction

The aim of this paper is to advise on the challenge of motivating students in an Academic Writing course. When teaching this course in the past, it was observed that students did not find academic writing very interesting. As a result, it was not very easy to sustain students' attention when they considered academic writing to be too formal and stodgy. In connection with this subject and its innovation, there were two problematic aspects which required a change – classes perceived by students as uninteresting and passive students. New assignments, useful practical exercises, homework and a variety in the types of papers to be written by students were considered as possible solutions. These will be discussed in this chapter.

At our school, Academic Writing is a compulsory course for all students in the first year of their bachelor degree. Students are required to attend one lecture per week which is given in Slovak language. The number of students depends on school enrolment. In the previous years it was about 30 students.

Academic writing is very important from a practical point of view, because studying at university requires students to produce good quality written works. According to Roter (2009: 96) there is generally one goal in any course on academic writing – to teach students how to write solid academic papers or to help them obtain the skill of academic writing.

Our department expects that this course will make new university students to write good papers concerning both their content and format. The course should make students learn to write different kinds of papers as well as their final thesis. High school graduates usually have no idea about academic writing, the rules of referencing or typography. Their papers tend to lack structure, argumentation and other criteria required for university level writing. In this innovation, two aims of academic writing were assigned: to introduce first year students to the appropriate ways of writing in an academic style, and to prepare them to write a variety of academic papers, including essays and the final thesis. Students learn the skills of writing good papers step-by-step.

The lectures in this course in the past usually consisted of the teacher's presentations about writing styles, plagiarism and the formal requirements.

However, talking about writing was not enough. Academic writing is a skills-driven course meaning that students were assigned homework, but the exercises were not sufficient. Students also had to hand in a seminar paper at the end of the semester. The final mark depended on both homework and the seminar paper. Unfortunately, the criteria were not enough specified in the syllabus. This was one of the reasons why the innovation was such a big challenge. As the person responsible for teaching this subject for two consecutive years, I had the opportunity to make some changes in the course design based on my previous experience in order to teach academic writing in a more effective way.

11.2 Aims of the Innovation and Theoretical Background

As the first part of this paper indicates, the reason for innovating teaching of academic writing was the fact that the lectures were not very interesting and students were passive. These problems occurred hand-in-hand with a lack of student motivation. According to Grofčíková (2007: 15), motivation is the way to make students more active, the lectures more dynamic and the educational process more regulated.

Kvasz (2005: 21) sees motivation as one of the key issues in education. He distinguishes between *external* and *internal motivation*. The first type of motivation is connected with potential stereotypes and possibilities of how to overcome this barrier. It is also important to emphasize that it is impossible to build a successful course solely on external motivation. According to Sullo (2007: 7), internal control psychology is based upon the belief that people are internally, not externally, motivated. The outside world, including all rewards and punishment, only provides us with information. It does not make us do anything. To summarize, students need external motivation, some kind of impulse from outside, but a good university course is one that tries to recapture also the internal motivation by compelling students to have some expectations for themselves.

Pintrich (2004: 395) mentions that *motivational self-regulatory strategies* include attempts to control self-efficacy through the use of positive self-talk; students also can attempt to increase their extrinsic motivation for the task by promising themselves extrinsic rewards or making certain positive activities.

Academic writing is considered by students to be unnecessary, because they think that process of writing is not so serious to require an extra course. This is the reason why motivating students seems very important. Students need an external impulse to awaken their interest. Activities with the aim to bring students into contact with writing are a kind of external motivation or external impulse, but students themselves should produce the purposes and interest to achieve them.

The theory of motivation is the base for this innovation, which had two aims – to make students more active and to make lectures more interesting and dynamic. It was necessary to change the structure of lectures and to motivate students, because motivated students are active students. Motivation seems to be a way to make students more active, but it is also a way to help students achieve better knowledge, and therefore better results. There is some connection with *Bloom's taxonomy* (Atherton 2011) that distinguishes between knowledge, comprehension, application, analysis, synthesis and evaluation. It was desirable to keep this in mind during the innovation and try to implement changes with reasonable seriousness which gave students the chance to experience all six levels of learning.

According to Roter (2009: 97), for the preparation of a course on academic writing, at least five internal factors appear particularly important: goals of the subject, students' previous knowledge, contents, exercise and teacher's workload. In addition to the factors that relate to the course itself, external factors also need to be taken into consideration such as: class size, technical issues and rules, and certain limitations within a particular academic environment. These facts were also very important for the innovation, which consisted of several steps to achieve the connection between external and internal motivation.

11.2.1 Reworked Syllabus

In connection with external motivation, a reworked syllabus and a more concrete, detailed and a more challenging system of assessment was the first step of the innovation. This was expected to make students more active during the semester, and make them participated in the creation of the classes. It was assumed that if students had to present their knowledge during the class, they had to be active, which could make classes more interesting and increase the quality of students' abilities thanks to the continuous study.

According to Morgan (2004: 215), learning outcomes should be part of the syllabus, because they signal clearly to students what they should be able to do upon completion of the course. In the case of the innovation for academic writing, there were three specified learning outcomes in the reworked syllabus: to write quality seminar papers and essays; to respect university guidelines, handbooks and other norms essential and useful in academic writing; to cite sources appropriately and to avoid plagiarism.

11.2.2 Restructured Concrete Topics in the Syllabus

To improve the academic writing class, it was necessary to restructure its topics in a more logical way. The process of writing is very important for topics order. When writing a paper, the authors should at first make a plan and outline as he or she is looking for literature and sources; then write the text followed usually by writing the introduction, conclusion, abstract and bibliography.

Previous year, the students did not try to work with external databases, because we mentioned the content aspect at the end of semester without any exercises or writing. It did not work very well. The importance of a having plan and the possibilities available in the university library should have been discussed at the beginning of the semester. First year students usually have no idea how to use external databases or how to search by key words in the library system or databases. Then, students should learn about the different types of papers (seminar paper, essay, final thesis) and their requirements (format, structure and extent). The content aspects of the papers (intention, clarity, expository practice, compositional units, lexical units, morphological and syntactical units) are also very important. Quotations and plagiarism should become the next topics. Then, at the end of semester, we should discuss guidelines for writing the introduction, abstract, conclusion and bibliography.

11.2.3 Attendance at Lectures and Continuous Assessment of Course-Work

Requirements for students' attendance were also a part of the innovation. As a new requirement, three or more absences meant failing the course. Students had compulsory consultations during office hours at least two times per semester.

11.2.4 Seminar Paper

Students had to hand in their seminar paper at the end of semester. Before, the criteria for the paper were not given in the syllabus. Roter (2009: 95) warns that students do not sufficiently or adequately cite their sources and often rely on non-academic sources such as Wikipedia. Therefore, students should become familiar with criteria for the use of literature.

In connection with the paper, three deadlines during the semester were specified. In the previous year, there was only one final deadline. This year's students worked step by step. For the first deadline, students proposed a topic they would like to write about, the list of sources they would use and the main ideas of their paper. For the second deadline, students handed in the first draft of their seminar paper. The third deadline was the date for the final version of their seminar paper.

11.2.5 Structure of Lessons

To make the students motivated and self-active, it was desirable to change the structure of classes as well. Teachers usually appreciate when students read materials before the lecture and demonstrate their knowledge, share information, participate in discussion or respond to questions. This was the reason why each student had to prepare some short information, notes about concrete topic, and present it to the rest of group once during the semester. All students had to read materials about the topic, but only one student had to present on it. After the presentation, there was an opportunity to ask questions, discussion and other activities.

If students had a presentation about a concrete topic, they had to consult about it with the teacher before the class. Feedback was offered in a written form – how students could improve their presentations, what information was missing, where some examples should have been supplemented or how to make the presentation more comprehensible.

11.3 Research Design

There were two possibilities for how to evaluate the effects of the innovation:

- To apply the innovative project only to chosen topics and compare them with topics learnt in the old way – to compare activity, attention and feedback of students, for example by minute paper;
- To compare the results of students from year 2011 with students from the previous year.

The second possibility, analysing the grades of two different cohorts, was chosen, along with teacher's observations on how students learnt under the new design. The arithmetic averages for the two groups – students in year 2010 and students in year 2011 were calculated. There are two arithmetic averages. The first one is for seminar papers and the second one for final marks. Final marks include seminar papers and exercises completed during the semester.

Students had to hand in the seminar papers at the end of semester. The requirement for passing the course was the same as the previous year. The method of seminar paper assessment was the same. It included two parts. First, the format of the seminar paper was assessed – meaning graphical and esthetical adjusting of the seminar paper and the language aspect of the seminar paper. Second, the content of the seminar paper was assessed – meaning the inclusion of the literature and the information sources, as well as the structure and method of elaboration of the seminar paper.

11.4 Findings

This was the first time that students had to read before lectures. In general, reading before lectures is not very popular among students, but from the teachers' point of view it is a chance for better understanding and better quality lectures based on discussion, which would not be possible without students' preparation. Some lectures ended with one-sentence summaries or minute papers. According to Angelo and Cross (1993: 148-183), the teacher can have students write one-sentence summaries expressing what they learned during the lecture. The minute paper means to stop the class a few minutes earlier and ask student to respond to one or two questions about lecture.

Students could realize what information was relevant and what they should have improved. It was also found an important way to start improving their writing skills and a way that the teacher could get feedback about students' knowledge. Thanks to the mentioned changes, the teacher did not have to lecture all the time, there was the time for discussion about materials and exercises and lessons were more interesting.

Because students submitted their papers in three deadlines, the teacher could give the students better feedback. Feedback could have been more detailed and more frequent, so students knew what improvements the teacher expected. For instance, if students chose very general themes, the teacher could note it in the feedback and students had the opportunity to specify their topics more clearly. Some tips for sources, the structure of the paper or stylistic suggestions were also found very useful. From the experience, the innovation caused a positive change in communication with students (an increase compared to the previous year). The students felt freer to ask for advice or opinions.

It was also found useful to encourage students to use foreign-language information sources as well as to put into practice everything said through some exercises or writing.

Consultations were a chance for students to ask questions about their activities, the seminar paper or others issues. It was assumed that problems or confusions could be promptly and clearly defined and solved through consultations. First year students often did not know about the chance for consultations and so this was a way to make them familiar with this possibility. Because first year students are sometimes shy to ask something in front of their peers it is easier for them to communicate with the teacher individually, which seems to be the reason why students' interest in consultation was really high.

In comparison to the students attending the course one year ago, this year's students had to do different exercises during the semester, which were believed to be more useful for them. The assessment of exercises during the semester influenced the resulting marks from both school years, which are presented in Table 4.

Table 4: Average marks for students by cohort.

	Academic year 2010/2011	Academic year 2011/2012
Seminar paper (SP)	2.89	2.15
Final mark (SP + exercises)	2.44	2.21

Source: own depiction

From the table (for which 1 is the highest achievable mark and 5 is the lowest mark), it is evident that students achieved better marks when they learnt under the innovated design. The arithmetic average for the seminar paper improved from 2.89 to 2.15, and in the case of the final mark from 2.44 to 2.21. But if the effect of exercises is compared, they influenced the final mark more dramatically one year ago, from 2.89 to 2.44. This year's exercises caused change from 2.15 to 2.21. We assume that exercises were quite easy in the previous year and following year's exercises were more challenging.

From the point of view of qualitative evaluation it is possible to say that papers were of better quality than one year ago. Students tried to use arguments to support their claims. There were not so many mistakes in citing and in the format of student papers.

It is also necessary to mention that motivating students of journalism – who have to write and publish journalistic articles – to shift to academic writing is not so easy. They are not as interested in academic writing because they prefer writing in the style required for newspapers. But it is important to add that this year's students were conscious of the importance of academic writing.

11.5 Limitations of the Study and Suggestions for Future Improvement

According to the numbers and arithmetic averages, we may say that there is some improvement thanks to the innovation; however, some possibilities still exist for improvement – such as including less theory and adding some more exercises and more writing during the semester.

The first problem during the innovation was related to the number of students and the length of lectures. Teaching a group of 32 students every week was quite demanding and sometimes the teacher was under pressure to give quality feedback on time. The lectures lasted only 45 minutes, so it was difficult to make sure if all students had read the material. It was impossible to ask the same question to everybody in the discussion and there was not enough time for one-sentence summaries at every lecture. A possible solution to this problem would be to change the lectures to 90 minutes which would be held fortnightly. It could provide more time for students' writing and for the teacher's feedback, but on the other hand it could imply less personal contact.

The second problem was that the rules were ignored by some students, especially those related to the seminar papers. In the syllabus, there was the condition to use at least three books, two reliable internet sources and at least two newspapers or magazines as sources. For the first deadline, students created a first version of their bibliography, which they could change or add to during the semester; however, in the final versions of their seminar papers, some students cited only one book, four websites and no newspapers. So ultimately, they were given worse marks. The reason why students broke the rule is not clear; perhaps they found some information sources useless for the final version of their seminar paper and so did not use any substitute book or magazine.

11.6 Conclusion

At our school, academic writing is a compulsory subject designed for students in the first year of their bachelor degree. The school requires students to produce good quality writings, so students must realize this fact and be challenged by the improved content and structure of the lessons.

The reason for innovation of the teaching the academic writing was the fact that lectures were not very interesting and students were passive. These problems occurred hand-in-hand with a lack of student motivation. To solve this problem it was necessary to clarify the passing requirements of the subject and to prepare useful number of homework and challenging exercises aimed at improving written skills of students. To evaluate the effect of the innovation, it was decided to compare the results of the students with the results from the previous year. It was found that students achieved better marks when they learnt using the innovated class design. From the point of view of the qualitative evaluation, the students' papers were much better and more professional than one year ago.

This innovation documented that some possibilities exist to motivate students and make them more active and interested in writing academic papers. This year's students had better knowledge and abilities than the students of previous year, especially thanks to exercises, homework and the way writing their final paper. Their papers improved both concerning content and formal aspects. As a result, there is an expectation that students will be able to write solid papers clearly and concisely.

References

Angelo, T. And Cross, P. (1993): Classroom Assessment Techniques: A Handbook for College Teachers. San Francisco: Jossey-Bass, pp. 148-183.

Atherton J. S. (2011) 'Bloom's taxonomy. ' In Learning and Teaching; Bloom's taxonomy. 7 March 2012, www.learningandteaching.info/learning/bloomtax.htm #ixzz29dve74ec.

Dunn, L./Morgan, C./O'Reilly, M./Parry, S. (2004): The Student Assessment Handbook. London: routledgefalmer.

Grofčíková S. (2007): "Učiteľ – motivácia – student." In: Pleschová G/Mattová I. (eds.): Ako kvalitne učiť? Skúsenosti začínajúcich VŠ učiteľov. Bratislava: Alternatíva Komunikácia Občania, pp. 15-16.

Kvasz, L. (2005): "On possible approaches to motivation." In: Gregušová, G. (ed.): How to Teach Political Science? The Experience of First-time University Teachers Teaching Political Science series no.1. Budapest: epsnet, pp. 21-26.

Pintrich R. P. (2004): "A conceptual framework for assessing motivation and self-regulated learning in college students." Educational Psychology Review, 16, 4, pp. 385-407.

Roter P. (2009): "Designing and teaching a course on Academic Writing: How can students learn the skill of writing?" In: Kas K./Brosig M. (eds.): From Teaching Theory and Academic Writing: A Guide to Undergraduate Lecturing in Political Science, pp. 95-106.

Sullo B. (2007): Activating the Desire to Learn. Alexandria: Association for Supervision & Curriculum Deve.

12. How to Change Teaching and Student Learning: Findings from Practice

Ľudmila Adamová, Petra Muráriková and Gabriela Pleschová

The purpose of this concluding chapter is to summarize the experience of innovating courses as part of the teacher development program *Teaching and Learning in Higher Education*. Teachers, who contributed to this book, decided to change their teaching and student learning in order to address the following challenges:

- Improving student pre-class preparation;
- Teaching large classes;
- Teaching courses rich in complex terminology;
- Enhancing student abilities of theory application;
- Making assessment an effective tool for student learning;
- Increasing student engagement.

In this chapter, teacher experience with overcoming these individual difficulties is compared and evaluated in order to provide examples and guidance for other instructors facing similar challenges.

12.1 Improving Student Pre-class Preparation

One of the main challenges the teachers faced was related to the insufficient pre-class preparation of their students, meaning that students were inadequately reading or not reading at all the assigned literature. If students fail to read before seminars, it is impossible to discuss and analyse the texts in class as well as to ask students to build upon their knowledge. One possible way to address this challenge is using the method of *just-in-time teaching* (Novak et al. 1999). Using this way, students are assigned to read some materials and to write a short essay or to answer a set of questions, which are submitted to the teacher before the class. The teacher then uses student responses and essays to initiate and facilitate in-class discussion and other learning activities. However, when using this method, it has proven essential to strictly follow the rules (described in the syllabus) and avoid accepting homework submitted after the deadline. This can be very important not only for making just-in-time teaching effective, but also for students to learn to respect given rules.

As another way to encourage student pre-class preparation, teachers can use self-scoring online quizzes. Also in this case students need to read the assigned literature first in order to familiarize themselves with the topic and terminology. But then, instead of writing an essay, students respond to a number of questions related to the texts. Using specialized software (for example Moodle) this method can be effectively used in courses with large number of students, as the software allows rapid evaluation of quiz results. The experience shows that taking and passing the quizzes should be compulsory, otherwise students may ignore this assignment or not answer the questions properly. In order to make this method work effectively, it can be advised that teachers pay attention to students who may try to circumvent the system. For example, students who attempt to collectively answer the questions can be detected by checking the time taken to complete the quiz (too short) or the time of quiz submission (simultaneous submissions).

Using the blogs can be another possible solution to missing student preparation. In this case students are assigned to write and upload a short article in the form of a blog (around 500 words) before their class. Because students' articles are read and commented on by their classmates and even the public, it provides a creative space for the exchange of ideas and opinions. Blogging motivates students to read and write and it can help them improve in critical reading and analytic thinking as well as in argumentation through confrontation with their peers' writing.

As the fourth method to improve student pre-class preparation, teachers can design special worksheets for students. Worksheets can consist of three main parts: a statement of the learning objectives to be achieved, a list of assigned readings and a problem set of exercises for practice. These worksheets can be distributed to students before each seminar (for example a week before) and students submit them with their answers before the class.

When using all these methods, it was found that designing seminar learning activities around the readings was important so that students could see a purpose in reading, and the teacher could further develop students' knowledge and skills. Using these different ways helps to return the seminars to their original purpose: to serve as forums of discussion, to promote learning in smaller groups and to develop knowledge acquired from literature and lectures instead of providing background knowledge to students by lecturing in the seminar.

12.2 Teaching Large Classes

Teaching large classes can be particularly challenging for teachers as it raises difficulties in encouraging more in-class participation, keeping students focused and providing enough attention to the needs of individual students, etc.

One way to teach large classes effectively is introducing the method of *problem solving groups* (Cohen 2008). This means dividing large groups of students into smaller ones and assigning each group a list with open-ended questions addressing the topic of the class. Ideally, for all questions different ways of approaching and answering the problem should be possible. By discussing various approaches in small groups, students can learn to better explain key concepts and apply their knowledge in practice. However, this innovation may fail to be effective unless the teacher manages to keep students motivated and active during the whole class/semester. Maintaining motivation can be achieved, for example, by linking this way of learning to the assessment.

Blended learning can become another solution. Here, the teacher engages students in learning not only during regular face-to-face classes but also in learning activities completed in a virtual learning environment. Instead of attending classes as one large group, students can be divided into two smaller groups, which alter their in-class and virtual classes every week.

A different method that can be employed for large student groups is *fill-in-the-blanks* activities. This method can be particularly effective if students have difficulty acquiring the necessary background knowledge from their lectures or textbook. Using this method, the teacher sends the students a lecture outline in advance that they bring to the lecture and then to the seminar. This can provide a frame with some keywords and definitions intentionally left out which students are asked to fill-in based on the lecture. This exercise can also help the teacher to identify issues misunderstood by students that should be further explored in the seminar.

12.3 Teaching Courses Rich in Complex Terminology

Teaching courses that require students to acquire complex terminology can be very demanding. This is often the case in foundational courses such as Anatomy or Plant Physiology, where students in the first years of study have difficulties coping with the rich terminology. Students typically try to use new terms but they are often not able to define them properly or see connections between facts they learn. In this case, *self-scoring online quizzes* can be helpful, because in using this method, students can quite effectively learn to define, explain and use new terminology.

In order to enhance long-term retention of terminology, teachers can use *associative learning and mnemonics* (Davies 2011). This method can also be applied, for example, in foreign languages courses.

Stimulation of active learning in students (Bonwell and Eison 1991) can be another way to help students with terminology. This includes activities aimed at enhancing their intrinsic motivation to learn, encouraging students' in-class engagement, developing cognitive competencies, and improving teamwork and the ability to accept constructive feedback. Various *learning games and competitions* as well as *project homework* can be used as tools of active learning. In using these activities, however, teachers need to pay attention to time management, as it can have an enormous impact on students' ability to cooperate and to take an active part. Aside from this, teachers should actively support students' participation and their engagement and provide students with regular feedback so that students can continuously improve.

12.4 Enhancing Student Abilities of Theory Application

One of the most frequent complaints made by students is that they are required to learn theory without appropriate illustration of its application in the "real world". Experience shows that if students can understand the alignment of theory and practice and if they can develop their application skills, this can lead to their increased engagement and development of skills, which is often more appreciated than achieving the best exam results.

One way to improve students' skills of theory application is Frank's approach (2005) grounded in helping students to process the information and to understand the subject matter in the *narrative form of stories*. For this purpose, teacher can create worksheets with learning objectives (to allow the students' to see the purpose of their learning), the assigned readings (to introduce the topic in an interest arousing and understandable way) and the problem set (to clearly and directly illustrate connection of theory and practice). Ideally, apart from using the worksheets, the teacher should stimulate students' continuous preparation for seminars and offer enough feedback.

Another way of teaching theory application can be asking students to regularly complete (e-) assignments, in which they can apply the theory that was presented earlier in lectures. The core of this innovation lies in the detailed and individualized teacher's feedback on each assignment. Although in using this method the quality of student work will continuously improve, it can be time demanding. As an alternative approach, teachers can use collective feedback either in the oral form or written form, for example by creating a feedback rubric with most frequently used comments and by checking only those comments that refer to the work of a particular student.

Students can also fail in theory application because they lack background knowledge. Again, *just-in-time teaching* can help students to obtain both theoretical background and learn theory application, if the assignments ask student to do both. To repeat, explicit rules and their respect from teacher as well as students is the key to successful accomplishment of this approach.

12.5 Making Assessment an Effective Tool for Student Learning

Sometimes it can happen that the course assessment does not wholly take advantage of its potential for students' learning. This can occur especially if the elements of the assessment are not well aligned with the learning outcomes and activities or if the assessment tasks do not fully address different levels of learning according to demands on students' cognitive activity. By making the activities and assessment tasks correspond to different levels of *Bloom's taxonomy*, teachers can avoid solely testing memorized facts. Aside from this by distributing the assessment tasks regularly throughout the semester, workload can be more appropriately distributed throughout the course. As a result, new assessment design can measure a broader area of skills and avoid overburdening both teachers and students.

Also, sometimes students can be discouraged by stereotypical assessments, particularly if they are always assessed using the same tasks. Here, bringing in some assessment formats not typically used in the department can result in a desired change of approach by students. When using some atypical assessment tasks, however, it is important that students have enough time to practice these tasks during the semester if they will later be used for their assessment.

Innovative teachers can find Cohen's (2008) categorization of three types of assessment useful. The *assessment of learning*, most frequently used, is usually realized by standard testing at the end of the semester. However, similarly important is the *assessment for learning* that is provided by the teacher's feedback on learning activities. Lastly, the *assessment as learning* can be based on students' self-assessment. The last two types of assessment help students to monitor their progress in learning and to increase their intrinsic motivation. The teacher, however, should be aware that complex assessment structure may cause confusion in students, at least initially.

Therefore, it is important to explain the assessment design to students in detail and regularly check if they understand its components and their purpose.

12.6 Increasing Student Engagement

Students' engagement, their attitudes and interest in learning, which rest on the core of the teaching and learning process, were addressed by most of the authors. Feeling a lack of deep engagement from students was one of the key challenges, and each of the teachers tried to identify its influences: the lack of students' enthusiasm to cooperate, seemingly uninteresting subject matters, stereotypical assessment design, lack of background knowledge, unclear presentation of connections between theory and practice, level of difficulty of course requirements and learning activities, the feeling of its redundancy within the curriculum and some others. As a consequence, students perceive the course as "a must", which prevents them from desired learning and skills development, which the course aims at.

As a way to increase student engagement, teachers can assign points for student in-class participation or incorporate interest-arousing stories into the curriculum. Experience has documented, however, that appropriate teaching style (centred on students and their learning rather than on teacher's performance, and involving regular feedback to students) and teachers' attitudes (showing genuine interest in students and their learning, demonstration of enthusiasm and commitment) can be far more motivating than other external motivational stimuli, such as assigning the points. If this way of motivation does not work, it can be recommended to seek reasons of student unenthusiasm from other sources, for example, in misunderstanding the task, in an inconvenient time schedule or in other factors.

The value of a course as seemingly useless in students' eyes can be another reason for their rather passive attitude in the classroom. In this case, it can be advised to use tools to increase both *intrinsic motivation* in students by trying to show them the subject as interesting and important as well as *external motivation* in students (Kvasz 2005), including for example changing the structure of classes, establishing a new, challenging system of assessment and creating new, fixed rules.

Another way to achieve students' engagement in the classroom is to improve student preparation. This type of approach can be a solution when the main reason for students' low involvement lies in their lack of background knowledge, which in fact leads to insufficient comprehension and hence to surface learning.

Last but not least, to enhance the enthusiasm of students, *blended learning* seems to be a promising tool. The expectation of its potential for motivation increase is rooted in the presupposition that students can benefit from the most common advantages attributed to blended learning, including its space and time flexibility, possibility for self-paced learning and the reduced number of personal meetings. Yet, it should be remembered, that no technology can substitute the vital part of a personal and devoted attitude of teachers to their students. Still, the willingness to offer a high level of personal inputs should be regulated by proper management of time, effort and interest on the teacher's part.

12.7 Findings from the Program

Contributions in this book document that teachers in the program made certain changes towards a student-centred approach to teaching but they have not yet become fully student-centred teachers. This can be seen, for example, in how some teachers continued to put stress on teaching rather than learning by frequently using the term *teaching*. Also, citations used in some teachers' reports (for example in Boleková) document teacher's focus on lecturing, knowledge acquisition and retention instead of on comprehension and application. Probably as a result of this, these teachers could not detect any significant differences between the results of students who had learnt in a new way and those students who had learnt in a traditional way.

On the other hand, in most reports attention to improved student learning as the ultimate purpose of teaching can clearly be detected, including above all an improved higher order thinking in students. The reports in this book document that in the course of one year, teachers can make some meaningful progress in the design of their classes, and moreover in their practice and in their thinking about teaching and student learning. However, more time is needed in order for teachers to become fully student-centred, reflective and critical about their teaching as well as to learn to use pedagogical theory as a tool for enhancing their practice, which were the aims of this teacher development program.

Aside from this, the reports document that teachers made their first steps in the field of scholarship of teaching and learning, i.e. They tried to use scholarly methods to evaluate the outcomes of their teaching and student learning, they derived from scholarly literature to put their results into the context and they published their findings.

The reports also offered valuable feedback for the design of the teacher development program. Some teachers reported an indirect way of evaluating the effects of innovation (feedback from students) where clearly the direct way would be appropriate (outcomes of student learning). In particular, one teacher asked students whether they think they did better on their test even though this was documented by their test results. Other teachers relied on student perceptions of their progress when quality of student work could have provided a more realistic picture of student progress. This approach was a result of teachers' missing background in methods of social science research and was not addressed enough during the teacher development program. In the follow-up summer school and teacher enquiry program it was decided to provide specific attention to this aspect of training.

12.8 Our Recommendations for Innovating Teachers

Changes that teachers participating in the teacher development program introduced into their courses revealed several dilemmas. For example, in order to improve student pre-class preparation, teachers oftentimes assigned students not only the readings but also certain questions to be answered based on the readings. However, literature reports this to be a risky approach, as it was found to encourage a surface approach to learning in students. When pre-assigned questions, students did not read the material with the aim of understanding it fully but instead chose to read only those parts that helped them to respond the questions which resulted in confusion and misunderstanding (Marton and Säljö 1976a,b).

Another argument against assigning the questions is the need to help students become independent learners. During the course of their studies, students should become able to formulate their own meaning from what they study, as well as to structure their knowledge themselves, instead of the teacher always being the guru who shapes student knowledge. Therefore, it can be recommended that teachers pre-assign questions to readers only in introductory classes when students struggle with making the meaning from complex texts. Alternately, teachers should carefully design a list of questions in a way that it always includes questions that require understanding of the purpose of the text, its methodology, connections between parts of the text, conclusions and their relationship with further literature.

Also, some contributors in this book tried to address the problem of low retention of knowledge in students. However, while in some courses, particularly in subjects like Medicine, focus on retention is important, we believe that this should not become the ultimate purpose of the innovation. After improving the remembering of facts, or better said, along with measures to improve remembering, teachers should strive to increase students' higher order thinking skills, including their abilities to compare, analyse, apply, design, etc.

Many of our teachers decided for innovation of their course because they felt worried by students being unengaged in class. Nevertheless, it must be stressed that improving student engagement should not be seen as the purpose of changed teaching. Instead, it is improved student learning and its outcomes, as many teachers themselves realized, that is the purpose of innovation. It is good news for all teachers who desire more enthusiastic students that designing and implementing innovation with the purpose of improved student learning mostly brings about also the desired increase in student engagement and overall enjoyment of the course both by teacher and students.

To address their teaching challenge, teachers in this book introduced a number of new learning activities for their students. However, many found that if the activity is repeated at each class, for example *a minute paper* or *the muddiest point*, it can become stereotypical for students, which results in decreased student engagement and lower inputs into completing the task. This calls for using different learning activities throughout the semester. On the other hand, students need some time to practice a new learning activity so that they can improve in completing it. Therefore, any new task should be repeated in several classes, for example three times a semester.

A number of teachers in this report (Valušová, Živčák, Adamová, Boleková) witnessed an improvement in student learning, as could be demonstrated by their own observations, examples of student work and student feedback. However, when considering student results, grades did not improve or even got worse when compared with previous year. These findings left teachers puzzled and could send an undesired message to their departments if interpreted as a failure of their innovation.

These results typically stemmed from the nature of an important component of the assessment. Even if teachers could sometimes change some components of the assessment, they were not authorized to change all its parts. Students were then assessed using a multiple choice questionnaire test or a written exam with numerous questions asking students mainly to remember and recall facts (i.e. To use surface approach to learning) instead of using their higher order thinking skills (i.e. Deep approach to learning). This part of the assessment was typically designed by a professor responsible for the whole course and was the same for students in different seminar groups taught by various teachers. This finding is consistent with what was earlier reported by Gibbs: if students who got used to approaching learning in a deep way are assessed using tasks that require surface approach to learning, they underperform their colleagues accustomed to using surface approach to learning (Gibbs 1992: 10, 167). Therefore, for making future innovations successful, one of the key challenges is for the innovating teachers to change or modify the assessment; otherwise, neither their students nor departments will feel a worthwhile stake in the teaching innovations.

Our further advice for teachers who think of introducing changes into their courses is consistent with earlier recommendations from literature (see Gibbs 1992: 171-172, Cowan 2006: 146-153). This includes:

– Design your changes in attune with pedagogic theory and with findings of other colleagues. This will give a rationale to your innovation, help you to clarify your expectations and avoid some difficulties already experienced by your forerunners.
– Avoid trying to change everything at once. Designing a change that requires what you do not have a capacity to influence will increase the risk of failure; moreover, it can stimulate aversion in students and if something goes wrong, you may not be able to isolate the cause. However, even when introducing a small change, it is necessary to provide that the principle of constructive alignment is respected (learning outcomes are in harmony with learning activities and assessment).
– Your small innovation can be a pilot for a more ambitious innovation in following semesters. We recommend changing courses step-by-step rather than making a big revolution in one year.
– Try to find support from some of your colleagues, including those teaching similar courses, more experienced teachers and colleagues with background in pedagogic theory, like for example the coaches in our program.
– Collect enough documentation on the impact of changes you introduced, including, for example, an innovation plan, new syllabus, examples of student work, responses from student surveys, copies of emails from students, results from interviews with students, summary of your observations (for example based on your teaching diary), summary of comments from your colleague (if you have invited anyone to observe and comment on your class), statistics of student results (grades), etc. Preferably, combine different sources of information when evaluating the results of your innovation in order to avoid bias stemming from using only one source.
– Publicize and publish results of your teaching. This would help you to receive useful comments on your findings, find new supportive colleagues, and develop your thinking about student learning. You can also inspire and advise other colleagues doing similar changes.

Finally, we wish you good luck with introducing changes into the way your students learn. And we would like to encourage you: even if your innovation does not fully meet your expectations, use your experience when further improving your course.

References

Bonwell, C. C./Eison, J. A. (1991): Active Learning: Creating Excitement in the Classroom. Higher Education Report No.1. George Washington University, Washington, DC: ASHEERIC Higher Education Report.

Cohen, M. (2008): "Participation as assessment: Political science and classroom assessment techniques." Political Science, 41, 3, pp. 609-612.

Cowan, J. (2011): On Becoming an Innovative University Teacher (2nd Edition). Blacklick, OH, USA: mcgraw-Hill Companies.

Davies, V. (2011): "Teaching and learning in higher education. How do people learn?' Handout from Summer school Teaching and Learning in Higher Education, Piešťany.

Frank, R. (2005): "Students Discover Economics in Its Natural State." 16 October 2012, www.nytimes.com/2005/09/29/business/29scene.html.

Gibbs, G. (1992): Improving the Quality of Student Learning. Bristol: Technical and Educational Services.

Kvasz, L. (2005): "On possible approaches to motivation." In: Gregušová, G. (ed.): How to Teach Political Science? How to Teach Political Science? The Experience of First-time University Teachers. Budapest: epsnet, pp. 21-26.

Marton F./Säljö, M. (1976a) "On Qualitative Differences in Learning 1: Outcome and Process." British Journal of Education Psychology, 46, pp. 4-11.

Marton F./Säljö, M. (1976b) "On Qualitative Differences in Learning 2: Outcome as a function of the learner's conception of the task." British Journal of Education Psychology, 46, pp. 115-127.

Novak, G./Gavrin, A./Christian, W./Patterson, E. (1999) Just-In-Time Teaching: Blending Active Learning with Web Technology. Upper Saddle River: Prentice Hall.

List of Contributors

Adamová Ľudmila
Department of English and American Studies, Constantine the Philosopher University in Nitra, ludmila.adamova@gmail.com

Boleková Adriana
Department of Anatomy, University of Pavol Jozef Šafárik in Košice, adriana.bolekova@upjs.sk

Dzurjaník Peter
Department of History, Constatine the Philosopher University in Nitra, pdzurjanik@ukf.sk, pdzurjanik@gmail.com

Hrnčiarová Katarína
Department of Philosophy and the History of Philosophy, University of Pavol Jozef Šafárik in Košice, kat.hrnciar@yahoo.com

Lučkaničová Martina
Department of Banking and Investment, Technical University of Košice, martina.luckanicova@tuke.sk

Muráriková Petra
Department of General and Applied Ethics, Constantine the Philosopher University in Nitra, petra.murarikova@gmail.com

Petáková Miroslava
Department of Journalism, Catholic University of Ružomberok, petakova.m@ku.sk

Pleschová Gabriela
Program Coordinator, Institute of Physics, Slovak Academy of Sciences, gabriela.pleschova@savba.sk

Repáňová Terézia
Department of Tourism and Hospitality, Matej Bel University in Banská Bystrica, terezia.repanova@gmail.com

Vallušová Anna
Department of Economics, Matej Bel University in Banská Bystrica, anna.vallusova@gmail.com

Živčák Marek
Department of Plant Physiology, Slovak University of Agriculture in Nitra, marek.zivcak@uniag.sk

Index